Christ Legends and other stories

Selma Lagerlöf

Christ Legends

and other stories

Floris Books

This arrangement first published
in English by Floris Books, 1977
Illustrations by G. & V. Knapp

The stories were originally published in Swedish.
The Holy Night, The Emperor's Vision, The Wise
Men's Well, Bethlehem's Children, The Flight into
Egypt, In Nazareth, In the Temple, Saint Veronica,
Robin Redbreast, The Sacred Flame from
Kristuslegender, © 1904 Selma Lagerlöf,
translated by Velma Swanston Howard. The Bird's
Nest from *Legender,* © 1894 Selma Lagerlöf,
translated by Pauline Bancroft Flach. The
Christmas Rose from *En Saga om en Sage,* © 1908
Selma Lagerlöf, translated by Velma Swanston
Howard.

This arrangement and illustrations © Floris Books,
21 Napier Road, Edinburgh, 1977.

ISBN 0 903540 06 1
Printed in Great Britain
by W. Blackwood & Sons Ltd., Edinburgh

Contents

The Holy Night

When I was five years old I had such a great sorrow! I hardly know if I have had a greater since.

It was then my grandmother died. Up to that time, she used to sit every day on the corner sofa in her room, and tell stories.

I remember that grandmother told story after story from morning till night, and that we children sat beside her, quite still, and listened. It was a glorious life! No other children had such happy times as we did.

It isn't much that I recollect about my grandmother. I remember that she had very beautiful snow-white hair, and stooped when she walked, and that she always sat and knitted a stocking.

And I even remember that when she had finished a story, she used to lay her hand on my head and say: "All this is as true, as true as that I see you and you see me."

I also remember that she could sing songs, but this she did not do every day. One of the songs was about a knight and a sea-troll, and had this refrain: "It blows cold, cold weather at sea."

Then I remember a little prayer she taught me, and a verse of a hymn.

Of all the stories she told me, I have but a dim and imperfect recollection. Only one of them do I remember so well that I should be able to repeat it. It is a little story about Jesus's birth.

Well, this is nearly all that I can recall about my grandmother, except the thing which I remember best; and that is, the great loneliness when she was gone.

I remember the morning when the corner sofa stood empty and when it was impossible to understand how the days would ever come to an end. That I remember. That I shall never forget!

And I recollect that we children were brought forward to kiss the hand of the dead and that we were afraid to do it. But then someone said to us that it would be the last time we could thank grandmother for all the pleasure she had given us.

And I remember how the stories and songs were driven from the homestead, shut up in a long black casket, and how they never came back again.

I remember that something was gone from our lives. It seemed as if the door to a whole beautiful, enchanted world — where before we had been free to go in and out — had been closed. And now there was no one who knew how to open that door.

And I remember that, little by little, we children learned to play with dolls and toys, and to live like other children. And then it seemed as though we no longer missed our grandmother, or remembered her.

But even today — after forty years — as I sit here and gather together the legends about Christ, which I heard out there in the Orient, there awakes within me the little legend of Jesus's birth that my grandmother used to tell, and I feel impelled to tell it once again, and to let it also be included in my collection.

It was a Christmas Day and all the folks had driven to church except grandmother and me. I believe we were all alone in the house. We had not been permitted to go along, because one of us was too old and the other was too young. And we were sad, both of us, because we had not been taken to early Mass to hear the singing and to see the Christmas candles.

But as we sat there in our loneliness, grandmother began to tell a story.

"There was a man," said she, "who went out in the dark night to borrow live coals to kindle a fire. He went from hut to hut and knocked.'Dear friends, help me!' said he. 'My wife has just given birth to a child, and I must make a fire to warm her and the little one.'

"But it was late in the night, and all the people were asleep. No one replied.

"The man walked and walked. At last he saw the gleam of a fire a long way off. Then he went in that direction, and saw that the fire was burning in the open. A lot of sheep were sleeping around the fire, and an old shepherd sat and watched over the flock.

"When the man who wanted to borrow fire came up to the sheep, he saw that three big dogs lay asleep at the shepherd's feet. All three awoke when the man approached and opened their great jaws, as though they wanted to bark; but not a sound was heard. The man noticed that the hair on their backs stood up and that their sharp, white teeth glistened in the firelight. They dashed toward him. He felt that one of them bit at his leg and one at his hand and that one clung to his throat. But their jaws and teeth wouldn't obey them, and the man didn't suffer the least harm.

"Now the man wished to go farther, to get what he needed. But the sheep lay back to back and so close to one another that he couldn't pass them. Then the man stepped upon their backs and walked over them and up to the fire. And not one of the animals awoke or moved."

Thus far, grandmother had been allowed to narrate without interruption. But at this point I couldn't help breaking in. "Why didn't they do it, grandma?" I asked.

"That you shall hear in a moment," said grandmother — and went on with her story.

9

"When the man had almost reached the fire, the shepherd looked up. He was a surly old man, who was unfriendly and harsh toward human beings. And when he saw the strange man coming he seized the long spiked staff, which he always held in his hand when he tended his flock, and threw it at him. The staff came right toward the man, but, before it reached him, it turned off to one side and whizzed past him, far out in the meadow."

When grandmother had got this far, I interrupted her again. "Grandma, why wouldn't the stick hurt the man?" Grandmother did not bother about answering me, but continued her story.

"Now the man came up to the shepherd and said to him: 'Good man, help me, and lend me a little fire! My wife has just given birth to a child, and I must make a fire to warm her and the little one.'

"The shepherd would rather have said no, but when he pondered that the dogs couldn't hurt the man, and the sheep had not run from him, and that the staff had not wished to strike him, he was a little afraid, and dared not deny the man that which he asked.

"'Take as much as you need!' he said to the man.

"But then the fire was nearly burnt out. There were no logs or branches left, only a big heap of live coals; and the stranger had neither spade nor shovel, wherein he could carry the red-hot coals.

"When the shepherd saw this, he said again: 'Take as much as you need!' And he was glad that the man wouldn't be able to take away any coals.

"But the man stooped and picked coals from the ashes with his bare hands, and laid them in his mantle. And he didn't burn his hands when he touched them, nor did the coals scorch his mantle; but he carried them away as if they had been nuts or apples."

But here the story-teller was interrupted for the third time. "Grandma, why wouldn't the coals burn the man?"

"That you shall hear," said grandmother, and went on. "And when the shepherd, who was such a cruel and hard-hearted man, saw all this, he began to wonder to himself: 'What kind of a night is this, when the dogs do not bite, the sheep are not scared, the staff does not kill, or the fire scorch?' He called the stranger back, and said to him: 'What kind of a night is this? And how does it happen that all things show you compassion?'

"Then said the man: 'I cannot tell you if you yourself do not see it.' And he wished to go his way, that he might soon make a fire and warm his wife and child.

"But the shepherd did not wish to lose sight of the man before he had found out what all this might portend. He got up and followed the man till they came to the place where he lived.

"Then the shepherd saw that the man didn't have so much as a hut to dwell in, but that his wife and babe were lying in a mountain grotto, where there was nothing except the cold and naked stone walls.

"But the shepherd thought that perhaps the poor innocent child might freeze to death there in the grotto; and, although he was a hard man, he was touched, and thought he would like to help it. And he loosened his knapsack from his shoulder, took from it a soft white sheepskin, gave it to the strange man, and said that he should let the child sleep on it.

"But just as soon as he showed that he, too, could be merciful, his eyes were opened, and he saw what he had not been able to see before and heard what he could not have heard before.

"He saw that all around him stood a ring of little silver-winged angels, and each held a stringed instrument, and all sang in loud tones that tonight the Saviour was born who should redeem the world from its sins.

"Then he understood how all things were so happy this night that they didn't want to do anything wrong.

"And it was not only around the shepherd that there were angels, but he saw them everywhere. They sat inside the grotto, they sat outside on the mountain, and they flew under the heavens. They came marching in great companies, and, as they passed, they paused and cast a glance at the child.

"There were such jubilation and such gladness and songs and play! And all this he saw in the dark night, whereas before he could not have made out anything. He was so happy because his eyes had been opened that he fell upon his knees and thanked God."

Here grandmother sighed and said: "What that shepherd saw we might also see, for the angels fly down from heaven every Christmas Eve, if we could only see them."

Then grandmother laid her hand on my head, and said: "You must remember this, for it is as true, as true as that I see you and you see me. It is not revealed by the light of lamps or candles, and it does not depend upon sun and moon; but that which is needful is, that we have such eyes as can see God's glory."

The Emperor's Vision

It happened at the time when Augustus was Emperor in Rome and Herod was King in Jerusalem.

It was then that a very great and holy night sank down over the earth. It was the darkest night that anyone had ever seen. One could have believed that the whole earth had fallen into a cellar-vault. It was impossible to distinguish water from land, and one could not find one's way on the most familiar road. And it couldn't be otherwise, for not a ray of light came from heaven. All the stars stayed at home in their own houses, and the fair moon held her face averted.

The silence and the stillness were as profound as the darkness. The rivers stood still in their courses, the wind did not stir, and even the aspen leaves had ceased to quiver. Had anyone walked along the seashore, he would have found that the waves no longer dashed upon the sands; and had one wandered in the desert, the sand would not have crunched under one's feet. Everything was as motionless as if turned to stone, so as not to disturb the holy night. The grass was afraid to grow, the dew could not fall, and the flowers dared not exhale their perfume.

On this night the wild beasts did not seek their prey, the serpents did not sting, and the dogs did not bark. And what was even more glorious, inanimate things would have been unwilling to disturb the night's sanctity, by lending themselves to an evil deed. No false key

14

could have picked a lock, and no knife could possibly have drawn a drop of blood.

In Rome, during this very night, a small company of people came from the Emperor's palace at the Palatine and took the path across the Forum which led to the Capitol. During the day which had just ended the Senators had asked the Emperor if he had any objections to their erecting a temple to him on Rome's sacred hill. But Augustus had not immediately given his consent. He did not know if it would be agreeable to the gods that he should own a temple next to theirs, and he had replied that first he wished to ascertain their will in the matter by offering a nocturnal sacrifice to his genius. It was he who, accompanied by a few trusted friends, was on his way to perform this sacrifice.

Augustus let them carry him in his litter, for he was old, and it was an effort for him to climb the long stairs leading to the Capitol. He himself held the cage with the doves for the sacrifice. No priests or soldiers or senators accompanied him, only his nearest friends. Torch-bearers walked in front of him in order to light the way in the night darkness and behind him followed the slaves, who carried the tripod, the knives, the charcoal, the sacred fire, and all the other things needed for the sacrifice.

On the way the Emperor chatted gaily with his faithful followers, and therefore none of them noticed the infinite silence and stillness of the night. Only when they had reached the highest point of the Capitol Hill and the vacant spot upon which they contemplated erecting the temple, did it dawn upon them that something unusual was taking place.

It could not be a night like all others, for up on the very edge of the cliff they saw the most remarkable being! At first they thought it was an old, distorted olive-trunk; later they imagined that an ancient stone figure from the temple of Jupiter had wandered out on the cliff.

15

Finally it was apparent to them that it could be only the old sibyl.

Anything so aged, so weather-beaten, and so giant-like in stature they had never seen. This old woman was awe-inspiring! If the Emperor had not been present, they would all have fled to their homes.

"It is she," they whispered to each other, "who has lived as many years as there are sand-grains on her native shores. Why has she come out from her cave just tonight? What does she foretell for the Emperor and the Empire — she, who writes her prophecies on the leaves of the trees and knows that the wind will carry the words of the oracle to the person for whom they are intended?"

They were so terrified that they would have dropped on their knees with their foreheads pressed against the earth, had the sibyl stirred. But she sat as still as though she were lifeless. Crouching upon the outermost edge of the cliff, and shading her eyes with her hand, she peered out into the night. She sat there as if she had gone up on the hill that she might see more clearly something that was happening far away. *She* could see things on a night like this!

At that moment the Emperor and all his retinue marked how profound the darkness was. None of them could see a hand's breadth in front of him. And what stillness! What silence! Not even the Tiber's hollow murmur could they hear. The air seemed to suffocate them, cold sweat broke out on their foreheads, and their hands were numb and powerless. They feared that some dreadful disaster was impending.

But no one cared to show that he was afraid, and everyone told the Emperor that this was a good omen. All Nature held its breath to greet a new god.

They counselled Augustus to hurry with the sacrifice, and said that the old sibyl had evidently come out of her cave to greet his genius.

But the truth was that the old sibyl was so absorbed in a vision that

she did not even know that Augustus had come up to the Capitol. She was transported in spirit to a far-distant land, where she imagined that she was wandering over a great plain. In the darkness she stubbed her foot continually against something, which she believed to be grass-tufts. She stooped down and felt with her hand. No, it was not grass, but sheep. She was walking between great sleeping flocks of sheep.

Then she noticed the shepherds' fire. It burned in the middle of the field, and she groped her way to it. The shepherds lay asleep by the fire, and beside them were the long, spiked staves with which they defended their flocks from wild beasts. But the little animals with the glittering eyes and the bushy tails that stole up to the fire, were they not jackals? And yet the shepherds did not fling their staves at them, the dogs continued to sleep, the sheep did not flee, and the wild animals lay down to rest beside the human beings.

This the sibyl saw, but she knew nothing of what was being enacted on the hill behind her. She did not know that they were raising an altar, lighting charcoal and strewing incense, and that the Emperor took one of the doves from the cage to sacrifice it. But his hands were so benumbed that he could not hold the bird. With one stroke of the wing, it freed itself and disappeared in the night darkness.

When this happened, the courtiers glanced suspiciously at the old sibyl. They believed that it was she who caused the misfortune.

Could they know that all the while the sibyl thought herself standing beside the shepherds' fire, and that she listened to a faint sound which came trembling through the dead-still night? She heard it long before she marked that it did not come from the earth, but from the sky. At last she raised her head; then she saw light, shimmering forms glide forward in the darkness. They were little flocks of angels, who, singing joyously, and apparently searching, flew back and forth above the wide plain.

While the sibyl was listening to the angel-song, the Emperor was making preparations for a new sacrifice. He washed his hands, cleansed the altar, and took up the other dove. And, although he exerted his full strength to hold it fast, the dove's slippery body slid from his hand, and the bird swung itself up into the impenetrable night.

The Emperor was appalled! He fell upon his knees and prayed to his genius. He implored him for strength to avert the disasters which this night seemed to foreshadow.

Nor did the sibyl hear any of this either. She was listening with her whole soul to the angel-song, which grew louder and louder. At last it became so powerful that it wakened the shepherds. They raised themselves on their elbows and saw shining hosts of silver-white angels move in the darkness in long, swaying lines, like migratory birds. Some held lutes and cymbals in their hands; others held zithers and harps, and their song rang out as merry as child-laughter, and as care-free as the lark's trill. When the shepherds heard this, they rose up to go to the mountain city, where they lived, to tell of the miracle.

They groped their way forward on a narrow, winding path, and the sibyl followed them. Suddenly it grew light up there on the mountain: a big, clear star kindled right over it, and the city on the mountain summit glittered like silver in the starlight. All the fluttering angel throngs hastened thither, shouting for joy, and the shepherds hurried so that they almost ran. When they reached the city, they found that the angels had assembled over a low stable near the city gate. It was a wretched structure, with a roof of straw and the naked cliff for a back wall. Over it hung the Star, and hither flocked more and more angels. Some seated themselves on the straw roof or alighted upon the steep mountain-wall behind the house; others, again, held themselves in the air on outspread wings, and hovered over it. High, high up, the air was illuminated by the shining wings.

The instant the Star kindled over the mountain city, all Nature awoke, and the men who stood upon Capitol Hill could not help seeing it. They felt fresh but caressing wings, which travelled through space; delicious perfumes streamed up about them; trees swayed; the Tiber began to murmur; the stars twinkled, and suddenly the moon stood out in the sky and lit up the world. And out of the clouds the two doves came circling down and lighted upon the Emperor's shoulders.

When this miracle happened, Augustus rose, proud and happy, but his friends and his slaves fell on their knees.

"Hail, Caesar!" they cried. "Thy genius has answered thee. Thou art the god who shall be worshipped on Capitol Hill!"

And this cry of homage, which the men in their transport gave as a tribute to the Emperor, was so loud that the old sibyl heard it. It waked her from her visions. She rose from her place on the edge of the cliff, and came down among the people. It was as if a dark cloud had arisen from the abyss and rushed down the mountain height. She was terrifying in her extreme age! Coarse hair hung in matted tangles around her head, her joints were enlarged, and the dark skin, hard as the bark of a tree, covered her body with furrow upon furrow.

Potent and awe-inspiring, she advanced toward the Emperor. With one hand she clutched his wrist, with the other she pointed toward the distant East.

"Look!" she commanded, and the Emperor raised his eyes and saw. The vaulted heavens opened before his eyes, and his glance travelled to the distant Orient. He saw a lowly stable behind a steep rock wall, and in the open doorway a few shepherds kneeling. Within the stable he saw a young mother on her knees before a little child, who lay upon a bundle of straw on the floor.

And the sibyl's big, knotty fingers pointed toward the poor babe. "Hail, Caesar!" cried the sibyl, in a burst of scornful laughter. "There is the god who shall be worshipped on Capitol Hill!"

Then Augustus shrank back from her, as from a maniac. But upon the sibyl fell the mighty spirit of prophecy. Her dim eyes began to burn, her hands were stretched toward heaven, her voice was so changed that it seemed not to be her own, but rang out with such resonance and power that it could have been heard over the whole world. And she uttered words which she appeared to be reading among the stars.

"Upon Capitol Hill shall Christ — the Redeemer of the world — be worshipped, but not frail mortals."

When she had said this, she strode past the terror-stricken men, walked slowly down the mountain, and disappeared.

But on the following day, Augustus strictly forbade the people to raise any temple to him on Capitol Hill. In place of it he built a sanctuary to the new-born God-Child, and called it HEAVEN'S ALTAR — *Ara Coeli*.

The Wise Men's Well

In old Judaea the Drought crept, gaunt and hollow-eyed, between shrunken thistles and yellowed grass.

It was summertime. The sun beat down upon the backs of unshaded hills, and the slightest breath of wind tore up thick clouds of lime dust from the greyish-white ground. The herds stood huddled together in the valleys, by the dried-up streams.

The Drought walked about and viewed the water supplies. He wandered over to Solomon's Pool, and sighed as he saw that they still held a small quantity of water from their mountain sources. Then he journeyed down to the famous David's Well, near Bethlehem, and found water even there. Finally, he tramped with shuffling gait toward the great highway which leads from Bethlehem to Jerusalem.

When he had arrived about half-way, he saw the Wise Men's Well, where it stands close by the roadside. He saw at a glance that it was almost dry. He seated himself on the curb, which consists of a single stone hollowed out, and looked into the well. The shining water-mirror, which usually was seen very near the opening, had sunk deep down, and the dirt and slime at the bottom of the well made it muddy and impure.

When the Well beheld the Drought's bronzed visage reflected in her clouded mirror, she shook with anguish.

"I wonder when you will be exhausted," said the Drought. "Surely, you do not expect to find any fresh water source, down there in the deep, to come and give you new life; and as for rain, God be praised! there can be no question of that for the next two or three months."

"You may rest content," sighed the Well, "for nothing can help me now. It would take no less than a well-spring from Paradise to save me!"

"Then I will not forsake you until every drop has been drained," said the Drought. He saw that the old Well was nearing its end, and now he wanted to have the pleasure of seeing it die out drop by drop.

He seated himself comfortably on the edge of the curb, and rejoiced as he heard how the Well sighed down there in the deep. He also took a keen delight in watching the thirsty wayfarers come up to the well-curb, let down the bucket, and draw it up again, with only a few drops of muddy water.

Thus the whole day passed; and when darkness descended, the Drought looked again into the Well. A little water still shimmered down there. "I'll stay here all night," cried he, "so do not hurry yourself! When it grows so light that I can look into you once more, I am certain that all will be over with you."

The Drought curled himself up on the edge of the well-curb, while the hot night, which was even more cruel, and more full of torment than the day had been, descended over Judaea. Dogs and jackals howled incessantly, and thirsty cows and asses answered them from their stuffy stalls.

When the breeze stirred a little now and then, it brought with it no relief, but was as hot and suffocating as a great sleeping monster's panting breath. The stars shone with the most resplendent brilliancy, and a little silvery new moon cast a pretty blue-green light over the grey hills. And in this light the Drought saw a great caravan come marching toward the hill where the Wise Men's Well was situated.

The Drought sat and gazed at the long procession, and rejoiced

again at the thought of all the thirst which was coming to the well, and would not find one drop of water with which to slake itself. There were so many animals and drivers they could easily have emptied the Well, even if it had been quite full. Suddenly he began to think there was something unusual, something ghost-like, about this caravan which came marching forward in the night. First, all the camels came within sight on a hill, which loomed up, high and distinct, against the horizon; it was as though they had stepped straight down from heaven. They also appeared to be larger than ordinary camels, and bore — all too lightly — the enormous burdens which weighted them.

Still he could not understand anything but that they were absolutely real, for to him they were just as plain as plain could be. He could even see that the three foremost animals were dromedaries, with grey, shiny skins; and that they were richly bridled and saddled, with fringed coverings, and were ridden by handsome, noble-looking knights.

The whole procession stopped at the well. With three sharp jerks, the dromedaries lay down on the ground, and their riders dismounted.

The pack-camels remained standing, and as they assembled they seemed to form a long line of necks and humps and peculiarly piled-up packs.

Immediately, the riders came up to the Drought and greeted him by laying their hands upon their foreheads and breasts. He saw that they wore dazzling white robes and huge turbans, on the front of each of which there was a clear, glittering star, which shone as if it had been taken direct from the skies.

"We come from a far-off land," said one of the strangers, "and we bid thee tell us if this is in truth the Wise Men's Well?"

"It is called so today," said the Drought, "but by tomorrow there will be no well here. It shall die tonight."

"I can understand this, as I see thee here," said the man. "But is not this one of the sacred wells, which never run dry? or whence has it derived its name?"

"I know it is sacred," said the Drought, "but what good will that do? The three wise men are in Paradise."

The three travellers exchanged glances. "Dost thou really know the history of this ancient well?" asked they.

"I know the history of all wells and fountains and brooks and rivers," said the Drought, with pride.

"Then grant us a pleasure, and tell us the story!" begged the strangers; and they seated themselves around the old enemy to all things growing, and listened.

The Drought shook himself and crawled up on the well-curb, like a story-teller upon his improvised throne, and began his tale.

"In Gebas, in Media, a city which lies near the border of the desert — and, therefore, it has often been a free and well-beloved city to me — there lived, many, many years ago, three men who were famed for their wisdom.

"They were also very poor, which was a most uncommon state of affairs; for, in Gebas, knowledge was held in high esteem, and was well recompensed. With these men, however, it could hardly have been otherwise, for one of them was very old, one was afflicted with leprosy, and the third was a black, thick-lipped negro. People regarded the first as much too old to teach them anything; the second they avoided for fear of contagion; and the third they would not listen to, because they thought they knew that no wisdom had ever come from Ethiopia.

"Meanwhile, the three wise ones became united through their common misery. They begged during the day at the same temple gate, and at night they slept on the same roof. In this way they at least had an opportunity to while away the hours, by meditating upon all the wonderful things which they observed in Nature and in the human race.

"One night, as they slept side by side on a roof, which was overgrown with stupefying red poppies, the eldest among them awoke; and hardly had he cast a glance around him, before he wakened the other two.

" 'Praised be our poverty, which compels us to sleep in the open!' he said to them. 'Awake! and raise your eyes to heaven!'

"Well," said the Drought, in a somewhat milder tone, "this was a night which no one who witnessed it can ever forget! The skies were so bright that the heavens, which usually resemble an arched vault, looked deep and transparent and full of waves, like a sea. The light surged backwards and forwards and the stars swam in their varying depths: some in among the light-waves; others upon the surface.

"But farthest away and highest up, the three men saw a faint shadow appear. This shadow travelled through space like a ball, and came nearer and nearer, and, as the ball approached, it began to brighten. But it brightened as roses do — may God let them all wither! — when they burst from their buds. It grew bigger and bigger, the dark cover about it turned back by degrees, and light broke forth on its sides into four distinct leaves. Finally, when it had descended to the nearest of the stars, it came to a standstill. Then the dark lobes uncurled themselves back and unfolded leaf upon leaf of beautiful, shimmering, rose-coloured light, until it was perfect, and shone like a star among the stars.

"When the poor men beheld this, their wisdom told them that at this moment a mighty king was born on earth: one, whose majesty and power should rise higher than that of Cyrus or of Alexander; and they said to one another: 'Let us go to the father and mother of the new-born babe and tell them what we have seen! Mayhap they will reward us with a purse of coin or a bracelet of gold.'

"They grasped their long travelling staves and went forth. They wandered through the city and out from the city gate; but there they felt doubtful for a moment as they saw before them the great stretch of dry, smooth desert, which human beings dread. Then they saw the new Star cast a narrow stream of light across the desert sand, and they wandered confidently forward with the star as their guide.

"All night long they tramped over the wide sand-plain, and throughout the entire journey they talked about the young, new-born king, whom they should find reposing in a cradle of gold, playing with precious stones. They whiled away the hours by talking

over how they should approach his father, the king, and his mother, the queen, and tell them that the heavens augured for their son power and beauty and joy, greater than Solomon's. They prided themselves upon the fact that God had called *them* to see the Star. They said to themselves that the parents of the new-born babe would not reward them with less than twenty purses of gold; perhaps they would give them so much gold that they no longer need suffer the pangs of poverty.

"I lay in wait on the desert like a lion," said the Drought, "and intended to throw myself upon these wanderers with all the agonies of thirst, but they eluded me. All night the Star had led them, and on the morrow, when the heavens brightened and all the other stars grew pale, it remained steady and illumined the desert and then guided them to an oasis where they found a spring and a ripe fruit-bearing tree. There they rested all that day. And towards night, as they saw the Star's rays border the sands, they went on.

"From the human way of looking at things," continued the Drought, "it was a delightful journey. The Star led them in such a way that they did not have to suffer either hunger or thirst. It led them past the sharp thistles, it avoided the thick, loose, flying sand; they escaped the burning sunshine and the hot desert storms. The three wise men said repeatedly to one another: 'God is protecting us and blessing our journey. We are His messengers.'

"Then, by degrees, they fell into my power," said the Drought. "These star-wanderers' hearts became transformed into as dry a desert as the one which they travelled through. They were filled with impotent pride and destructive greed.

"'We are God's messengers!' repeated the three wise ones. 'The father of the new-born king will not reward us too well, even if he gives us a caravan laden with gold.'

"By and by, the Star led them over the far-famed River Jordan, and

30

up among the hills of Judaea. One night it stood still over the little city of Bethlehem, which lay upon a hill-top, and shone among the olive trees.

"But the three wise ones looked around for castles and fortified towers and walls, and all the other things that belong to a royal city; but of such they saw nothing. And what was still worse, the Star's light did not even lead them into the city but remained over a grotto near the wayside. There, the soft light stole in through the opening and revealed to the three wanderers a little Child, who was being lulled to sleep in its mother's arms.

"Although the three men saw how the Star's light encircled the Child's head, like a crown, they remained standing outside the grotto. They did not enter to prophesy honours and kingdoms for this little One. They turned away without betraying their presence. They fled from the Child, and wandered down the hill again.

" 'Have we come in search of beggars as poor as ourselves?' said they. 'Has God brought us hither that we might mock Him, and predict honours for a shepherd's son? This Child will never attain any higher distinction than to tend sheep here in the valleys'."

The Drought chuckled to himself and nodded to his hearers, as much as to say: "Am I not right? There are things which are drier than the desert stands, but there is nothing more barren than the human heart."

"The three wise ones had not wandered very far before they thought they had gone astray and had not followed the Star rightly," continued the Drought. "They turned their gaze upward to find again the Star, and the right road; but then the Star which they had followed all the way from the Orient had vanished from the heavens."

The three strangers made a quick movement, and their faces expressed deep suffering.

"That which now happened," continued the Drought, "is in accord with the usual manner of mankind in judging of what is, perhaps, a blessing.

"To be sure, when the three wise men no longer saw the Star, they understood at once that they had sinned against God.

"And it happened with them," continued the Drought furiously, "just as it happens with the ground in the autumn, when the heavy rains begin to fall. They shook with terror, as one shakes when it thunders and lightens; their whole being softened, and humility, like green grass sprang up in their souls.

"For three nights and days they wandered about the country, in quest of the Child whom they would worship; but the Star did not appear to them. They grew more and more bewildered, and suffered the most overwhelming anguish and despair. On the third day they came to this well to drink. Then God had pardoned their sin. And, as they bent over the water, they saw in its depths the reflection of the Star which had brought them from the Orient. Instantly they saw it also in the heavens and it led them again to the grotto in Bethlehem, where they fell upon their knees before the Child and said: 'We bring thee golden vessels filled with incense and costly spices. Thou shalt be the greatest king that ever lived upon earth, from its creation even unto its destruction.'

"Then the Child laid his hand upon their lowered heads, and when they rose, lo! the Child had given them gifts greater than a king could have granted; for the old beggar had grown young, the leper was made whole, and the negro was transformed into a beautiful white man. And it is said of them that they were glorious and that they departed and became kings — each in his own kingdom."

The Drought paused in his story, and the three strangers praised it. "Thou hast spoken well," said they. "But it surprises me," said one of them, "that the three wise men do nothing for the well which showed them the Star. Shall they entirely forget such a great blessing?"

"Should not this well remain perpetually," said the second stranger, "to remind mankind that happiness, which is lost on the heights of pride and vainglory, will let itself be found again in the depths of humility?"

"Are the departed worse than the living?" asked the third. "Does gratitude die with those who live in Paradise?"

But as he heard this, the Drought sprang up with a wild cry. He had recognized the strangers! He understood who the strangers were, and fled from them like a madman, that he might not witness how the Three Wise Men called their servants and led their camels, laden with water-sacks, to the Well and filled the poor dying Well with water, which they had brought with them from Paradise.

Bethlehem's Children

Just outside the Bethlehem gate stood a Roman soldier, on guard. He was arrayed in full armour, with helmet. At his side he wore a short sword, and held in his hand a long spear. He stood there all day almost motionless, so that one could readily have believed him to be a man made of iron. The city people went in and out of the gate and beggars lolled in the shade under the archway, fruit vendors and wine dealers set their baskets and jugs down on the ground beside the soldier, but he scarcely took the trouble to turn his head to look at them.

It seemed as though he wanted to say: This is nothing to see. What do I care about you who labour and barter and come driving with oil casks and wine sacks! Let me see an army prepare to meet the enemy! Let me see the excitement and the hot struggle, when horsemen charge down upon a troop of foot-soldiers! Let me see the brave men who rush forward to scale the walls of a beleaguered city! Nothing is pleasing to my sight but war. I long to see the Roman Eagles glisten in the air! I long for the trumpets' blast, for shining weapons, for the splash of red blood!

Just beyond the city gate lay a fine meadow, overgrown with lilies. Day by day the soldier stood with his eyes turned toward this meadow, but never for a moment did he think of admiring the extraordinary beauty of the flowers. Sometimes he noticed that the passers-by stopped to admire the lilies, and it amazed him to think that people would delay their travels to look at anything so trivial. These people did not know what is beautiful, thought he.

And as he thought thus, he saw no more the green fields and olive groves round about Bethlehem; but dreamed himself away in a burning-hot desert in sunny Libya. He saw a legion of soldiers march forward in a long, straight line over the yellow, trackless sand. There was no protection against the sun's piercing rays, no cooling stream, no apparent boundaries to the desert, and no goal in sight, no end to their wanderings. He saw soldiers, exhausted by hunger and thirst, march forward with faltering step; he saw one after another drop to the ground, overcome by the scorching heat. Nevertheless, they marched onward without a murmur, without a thought of deserting their leader and turning back.

Now, *there* is something beautiful! thought the soldier, something that is worth the glance of a valiant man!

Since the soldier stood on guard at the same post day after day, he had the best opportunity to watch the pretty children who played about him. But it was with the children as with the flowers: he didn't understand that it could be worth his while to notice them. What is this to rejoice over? thought he, when he saw people smile as they watched the children's games. It is strange that any one can find pleasure in a mere nothing.

One day when the soldier was standing at his accustomed post, he saw a little boy about three years old come out on the meadow to play. He was a poor lad, who was dressed in a scanty sheepskin, and who played quite by himself. The soldier stood and regarded the newcomer almost without being aware of it himself. The first thing that attracted him was that the little one ran so lightly over the field that he seemed scarcely to touch the tips of the grass-blades. Later, as he followed the child's play, he was even more astonished. "By my sword!'' he exclaimed, ''this child does not play like the others. What can it be that occupies him?''

As the child played only a few paces away, he could see well enough what the little one was doing. He saw how he reached out his hand to capture a bee that sat upon the edge of a flower and was so heavily laden with pollen that it could hardly lift its wings for flight. He saw, to his great surprise, that the bee let itself be taken without trying to escape, and without using its sting. When the little one held the bee secure between his fingers, he ran over to a crack in the city wall, where a swarm of bees had their home, and set the bee down. As soon as he had helped one bee in this way, he hastened

back to help another. All day long the soldier saw him catch bees and carry them to their home.

"That boy is certainly more foolish than any I've seen hitherto," thought the soldier. "What put it into his head to try and help these bees, who can take such good care of themselves without him, and who can sting him at that? What kind of a man will he become if he lives, I wonder?"

The little one came back day after day and played in the meadow, and the soldier couldn't help marvelling at him and his games.

"It is very strange," thought he. "Here I have stood on guard for fully three years, and thus far I have seen nothing that could interest me, except this infant."

But the soldier was in nowise pleased with the child; quite the reverse! For this child reminded him of a dreadful prediction made by an old Hebrew seer, who had prophesied that a time of peace should come to this world some day; during a period of a thousand years no blood would be shed, no wars waged, but human beings would love one another like brethren. When the soldier thought that anything so dreadful might really come to pass, a shudder passed through his body, and he gripped his spear hard, as if he sought support.

And now, the more the soldier saw of the little one and his play, the more he thought of the Thousand-year Reign of Peace. He did not fear that it had come already, but he did not like to be reminded of anything so hateful!

One day, when the little one was playing among the flowers on the pretty meadow, a very heavy shower came bursting through the clouds. When he noticed how big and heavy the drops were that beat down upon the sensitive lilies, he seemed anxious for his pretty friends. He hurried away to the biggest and loveliest among them, and bent towards the ground the stiff stalk which held up the lily, so that the raindrops caught the chalices on their under side. As soon as he had treated one flower like this, he ran to another and bent its stem in the same way, so that the flower-cups were turned toward the ground. And then to a third and a fourth, until all the flowers in the meadow were protected against the rainfall.

The soldier smiled to himself when he saw the boy's work. "I'm afraid the lilies won't thank him for this," said he. "Naturally, every stalk is broken. It won't do to bend such stiff growths in that way!"

But when the shower was over, the soldier saw the little lad hurry over to the lilies and raise them up. To his utter astonishment, the boy straightened the stiff stalks without the least difficulty. It was apparent that not one of them was either broken or bruised. He ran from flower to flower, and soon all the rescued lilies shone in their full splendour in the meadow.

When the soldier saw this, he was seized with a singular rage. "What a queer child!" thought he. "It is incredible that he can undertake anything so idiotic. What kind of man will he make, who cannot even bear to see a lily destroyed? How would it turn out if such a one had to go to war? What would he do if they ordered him to burn a house filled with women and children, or to sink a ship with all souls on board?"

Again he thought of the old prophecy, and he began to fear that the time had actually come for its fulfilment. "Since a child like this is here," thought he, "perhaps this awful time is very close at hand. Already, peace prevails over the whole earth; and surely the day of war will nevermore dawn. From this time forth, all peoples will be of the same mind as this child: they will be afraid to injure one another, yea, they will not have the heart even to crush a bee or a flower! No great deeds will be done, no glorious battles won, and no brilliant triumvirate will march up to the Capitol. Nothing more will happen that a brave man could long for."

And the soldier — who all the while hoped he would soon live through new wars and longed, through daring feats, to raise himself to power and riches — felt so exasperated with the little three-year-old that he raised his spear threateningly the next time the child ran past.

Another day it was neither the bees nor the lilies the little one sought to protect, but he undertook something which struck the soldier as being much more needless and thankless.

It was a fearfully hot day, and the sunrays fell upon the soldier's helmet and armour and heated them until he felt as if he wore a suit of fire. To the passers-by it looked as if he must suffer tortures from the heat. His bloodshot eyes were ready to burst from their sockets, and his lips were dry and shrivelled. But as he was inured to the burning heat of African deserts, he thought this a mere trifle, and it didn't occur to him to move from his accustomed place. On the contrary he took pleasure in showing the passers-by that he was so strong and hardy and did not need to seek shelter from the sun.

While he stood thus, and let himself be nearly broiled alive, the little boy who was wont to play in the meadow came suddenly up to him. He knew very well that the soldier was not one of his friends and so he was always careful not to come within reach of his spear; but now he ran up to him, and regarded him long and carefully; then he hurried as fast as he could towards the road. When he came back, he held both hands like a bowl, and carried in this way a few drops of water.

"Mayhap this infant has taken it upon himself to run and fetch water for me," thought the soldier. "He is certainly wanting in common sense. Should not a Roman soldier be able to stand a little heat! What need for that youngster to run around and help those who require no help! I don't want his compassion. I wish he and all like him were out of the world!"

39

The little one came walking very slowly. He held his fingers close together, so that nothing should be spilled or wasted. All the while, as he was nearing the soldier, he kept his eyes anxiously fixed upon the little water which he brought with him, and did not see that the man stood there frowning, with a forbidding look in his eye. Then the child came up to the soldier and offered him the water.

On the way his heavy blond curls had tumbled down over his forehead and eyes. He shook his head several times to get the hair out of his eyes, so that he could look up. When he succeeded at last, and became conscious of the hard expression on the soldier's face, he was not frightened, but stood still and begged him, with a bewitching smile, to taste of the water which he had brought with him. But the soldier felt no desire to accept a kindness from the child, whom he regarded as his enemy. He did not look down into his pretty face, but stood rigid and immovable, and showed no sign that he understood what the child wished to do for him.

Nor could the child understand that the man wished to repel him. He smiled all the while just as confidently, raised himself on the tips of his toes, and stretched his hands as high as he could that the big soldier might more easily get at the water.

The soldier felt so insulted because a mere child wished to help him that he gripped his spear to drive the little one away.

But just at that moment the extreme heat and sunshine beat down upon the soldier with such intensity that he saw red flames dance before his eyes and felt his brains melt within his head. He feared the sun would kill him, if he could not find instant relief.

Beside himself with terror at the danger hovering over him, the soldier threw his spear on the ground, seized the child with both hands, lifted him up, and absorbed as much as he could of the water which the little one held in his hands.

Only a few drops touched his tongue, but more was not needed.

40

As soon as he had tasted of the water, a delicious coolness surged through his body, and he felt no more that the helmet and armour burnt and oppressed him. The sunrays had lost their deadly power. His dry lips became soft and moist again, and red flames no longer danced before his eyes.

Before he had time to realize all this, he had already put down the child, who ran back to the meadow to play. Astonished, the soldier began to say to himself: "What kind of water was this that the child gave me? It was a glorious drink! I must really show him my gratitude."

But inasmuch as he hated the little one, he soon dismissed this idea. "It is only a child," thought he, "and does not know why he acts in this way or that way. He plays only the play that pleases him best. Does he perhaps receive any gratitude from the bees or the lilies? On that youngster's account I need give myself no trouble. He doesn't even know that he has succoured me."

The soldier felt, if possible, even more exasperated with the child a moment later, when he saw the commander of the Roman soldiers, who were encamped in Bethlehem, come out through the gate. "Just see what a risk I have run through that little one's rash behaviour!" thought he. "If by chance Voltigius had come a moment earlier, he would have seen me standing with a child in my arms."

Meanwhile, the Commander walked straight up to the soldier and asked him if they might speak together there without danger of being overheard. He had a secret to impart to him. "If we move ten paces from the gate," replied the soldier, "no one can hear us."

"You know," said the Commander, "that King Herod, time and again, has tried to get possession of a child that is growing up here in Bethlehem. His soothsayers and priests have told him that this child shall ascend his throne. Moreover, they have predicted that the new King will inaugurate a thousand-year reign of peace and holiness.

You understand, of course, that Herod would willingly make him — harmless!"

"I understand!" said the soldier eagerly. "But that ought to be the easiest thing in the world."

"It would certainly be very easy," said the Commander, "if the King only knew which one of all the children here in Bethlehem is the one."

The soldier knit his brows. "It is a pity his soothsayers cannot enlighten him about this," said he.

"But now Herod has hit upon a ruse, whereby he believes he can make the young Peace-Prince harmless," continued the Commander. "He promises a handsome gift to each and all who will help him."

"Whatsoever Voltigius commands shall be carried out, even without money or gifts," said the soldier.

"I thank you," replied the Commander. "Listen, now, to the King's plan! He intends to celebrate the birthday of his youngest son by arranging a festival, to which all male children in Bethlehem, who are between the ages of two and three years, shall be bidden, together with their mothers. And during this festival —— " He checked himself suddenly, and laughed when he saw the look of disgust on the soldier's face.

"My friend," he continued, "you need not fear that Herod thinks of using us as child-nurses. Now bend your ear to my mouth, and I'll confide to you his design."

The Commander whispered long with the soldier, and when he had disclosed all, he said: "I need hardly tell you that absolute silence is imperative, lest the whole undertaking miscarry."

"You know, Voltigius, that you can rely on me," said the soldier.

When the Commander had gone and the soldier once more stood alone at his post, he looked around for the child. The little one

42

played all the while among the flowers, and the soldier caught himself thinking that the boy swayed above them as light and attractive as a butterfly.

Suddenly he began to laugh. "True," said he, "I shall not have to vex myself very long over this child. He shall be bidden to the feast of Herod this evening."

He remained at his post all that day, until the even was come, and it was time to close the city gate for the night.

When this was done, he wandered through narrow and dark streets, to a splendid palace which Herod owned in Bethlehem.

In the centre of this immense palace was a large stone-paved court encircled by buildings, around which ran three open galleries, one above the other. The King had ordered that the festival for the Bethlehem children should be held on the uppermost of these galleries.

This gallery, by the King's express command, was transformed so that it looked like a covered walk in a beautiful flower-garden. The ceiling was hidden by creeping vines hung with thick clusters of luscious grapes, and alongside the walls, and against the pillars stood small pomegranate trees, laden with ripe fruit. The floors were strewn with rose-leaves, lying thick and soft like a carpet. And all along the balustrades, the cornices, the tables, and the low divans, ran garlands of lustrous white lilies.

Here and there in this flower-garden stood great marble basins, where glittering gold and silver fish played in the transparent water. Multi-coloured birds from distant lands sat in the trees, and in a cage sat an old raven that chattered incessantly.

When the festival began children and mothers filed into the gallery. Immediately after they had entered the palace, the children were arrayed in white dresses with purple borders, and were given wreaths of roses for their dark, curly heads. The women came in,

43

regal in their crimson and blue robes, and their white veils, which hung in long, loose folds from high-peaked head-dresses, adorned with gold coins and chains. Some carried their children mounted upon their shoulders, others led their sons by the hand, some again, whose children were afraid or shy, had taken them up in their arms.

The women seated themselves on the floor of the gallery. As soon as they had taken their places, slaves came in and placed before them low tables, which they spread with the choicest food and wines — as befitting a King's feast — and all these happy mothers began to eat and drink, maintaining all the while that proud, graceful dignity, which is the greatest ornament of the Bethlehem women.

44

Along the farthest wall of the gallery, and almost hidden by flower-garlands and fruit trees, was stationed a double line of soldiers in full armour. They stood, perfectly immovable, as if they had no concern with that which went on around them. The women could not refrain from casting a questioning glance, now and then, at this troop of iron-clad men. "For what are they needed here?" they whispered. "Does Herod think we women do not know how to conduct ourselves? Does he believe it is necessary for so many soldiers to guard us?"

But others whispered that this was as it should be in a King's home. Herod himself never gave a banquet without having his house filled with soldiers. It was to honour them that the heavily armoured warriors stood there on guard.

During the first few moments of the feast, the children felt timid and uncertain, and sat quietly beside their mothers. But soon they began to move about and take possession of all the good things which Herod offered them.

It was an enchanted land that the King had created for his little guests. When they wandered through the gallery, they found bee-hives whose honey they could pillage without the interference of a single crotchety bee. They found trees which, bending, lowered their fruit-laden branches down to them. In a corner they found magicians who, on the instant, conjured their pockets full of toys, and in another corner they discovered a wild-beast tamer who showed them a pair of tigers, so tame that they could ride them.

But in this paradise with all its joys there was nothing which so attracted the attention of these little ones as the long line of soldiers who stood immovable at the extreme end of the gallery. Their eyes were captivated by their shining helmets, their stern, haughty faces, and their short swords, which reposed in richly jewelled sheaths.

All the while, as they played and romped with one another, they thought continually about the soldiers. They still held themselves at a distance, but they longed to get near the men to see if they were alive and really could move themselves.

The play and festivities increased every moment, but the soldiers stood all the while immovable. It seemed incredible to the little ones that people could stand so near the clusters of grapes and all the other dainties, without reaching out a hand to take them.

Finally, there was one boy who couldn't restrain his curiosity any longer. Slowly, but prepared for hasty retreat, he approached one of the armoured men; and when he remained just as rigid and motion-less, the child came nearer and nearer. At last he was so close to him that he could touch his shoe latchets and his shins.

Then — as though this had been an unheard-of crime — all at once those iron-men set themselves in motion. With indescribable fury they threw themselves upon the children, and seized them! Some swung them over their heads, like missiles, and flung them between lamps and garlands over the balustrade and down to the court, where they were killed the instant they struck the stone pavement. Others drew their swords and pierced the children's hearts; others, again, crushed their heads against the walls before they threw them down into the dark courtyard.

The first moment after the onslaught, there was an ominous still-ness. While the tiny bodies still swayed in the air, the women were petrified with amazement! But simultaneously all these unhappy mothers awoke to understand what had happened, and with one great cry they rushed toward the soldiers. There were still a few children left up in the gallery who had not been captured during the first attack. The soldiers pursued them and their mothers threw themselves in front of them and clutched with bare hands the naked swords, to avert the death-blow. Several women, whose children were already dead, threw themselves upon the soldiers, clutched them by the throat, and sought to avenge the death of their little ones by strangling their murderers.

During this wild confusion, while fearful shrieks rang through the palace, and the most inhuman death cruelties were being enacted, the soldier who was wont to stand on guard at the city gate stood motionless at the head of the stairs which led down from the gallery. He took no part in the strife and the murder: only against the women who had succeeded in snatching their children and tried to fly down the stairs with them did he lift his sword. And just the sight of him, where he stood, grim and inflexible, was so terrifying that the fleeing ones chose rather to cast themselves over the balustrade or turn back into the heat of the struggle, than risk the danger of crowding past him.

"Voltigius certainly did the right thing when he gave *me* this post," thought the soldier. "A young and thoughtless warrior would have left his place and rushed into the confusion. If I had let myself be tempted away from here, ten children at least would have escaped."

While he was thinking of this, a young woman, who had snatched up her child, came rushing towards him in hurried flight. None of the warriors whom she had to pass could stop her, because they were in the midst of the struggle with other women, and in this way she had reached the end of the gallery.

"Ah, there's one who is about to escape!" thought the soldier. "Neither she nor the child is wounded."

The woman came toward the soldier with such speed that she appeared to be flying, and he didn't have time to distinguish the features of either the woman or her child. He only pointed his sword at them, and the woman, with the child in her arms, dashed against it. He expected that the next second both she and the child would fall to the ground pierced through and through.

But just then the soldier heard an angry buzzing over his head, and the next instant he felt a sharp pain in one eye. It was so intense that he was stunned, bewildered, and the sword dropped from his hand. He raised his hand to his eye and caught hold of a bee, and understood that that which caused this awful suffering was only the sting of the tiny creature. Quick as a flash, he stooped down and picked up the sword, in the hope that as yet it was not too late to intercept the runaways.

But the little bee had done its work very well.

During the short time that the soldier was blinded, the young mother had succeeded in rushing past him and down the stairs; and although he hurried after her with all haste, he could not find her. She had vanished; and in all that great palace there was no one who could discover any trace of her.

The following morning, the soldier, together with several of his comrades, stood on guard, just within the city gate. The hour was early, and the city gates had only just been opened. But it appeared as though no one had expected that they would be opened that morning; for no throngs of field labourers streamed out of the city, as they usually did of a morning. All the Bethlehem inhabitants were so filled with terror over the night's bloodshed that no one dared to leave his home.

"By my sword!" said the soldier, as he stood and stared down the narrow street which led toward the gate, "I believe Voltigius has made a stupid blunder. It would have been better had he kept the gates closed and ordered a thorough search of every house in the city, until he had found the boy who managed to escape from the feast. Voltigius expects that his parents will try to get him away from here as soon as they learn that the gates are open. I fear this is not a wise calculation. How easily they could conceal a child!"

He wondered if they would try to hide the child in a fruit basket or in some huge oil cask, or amongst the grain-bales of a caravan.

While he stood there on the watch for any attempt to deceive him in this way, he saw a man and a woman who came hurriedly down the street and were nearing the gate. They walked rapidly and cast anxious looks behind them, as though they were fleeing from some danger. The man held an axe in his hand with a firm grip, as if determined to fight should any one bar his way. But the soldier did not look at the man as much as he did at the woman. He thought that she was just as tall as the young mother who got away from him the night before. He observed also that she had thrown her skirt over her head. "Perhaps she wears it like this," thought he, "To conceal the fact that she holds a child on her arm."

The nearer they approached, the plainer he saw the child which the woman bore in her arm outlined under the raised robe. "I'm positive it is the one who got away last night. I didn't see her face, but I recognize the tall figure. And here she comes now, with the child on her arm, and without even trying to keep it concealed. I had not dared to hope for such a lucky chance," said the soldier to himself.

The man and woman continued their rapid pace all the way to the city gate. Evidently, they had not anticipated being intercepted here. They trembled with fright when the soldier levelled his spear at them, and barred their passage.

"Why do you refuse to let us go out in the fields to our work?" asked the man.

"You may go presently," said the soldier, "but first I must see what your wife has hidden behind her robe."

"What is there to see?" said the man. "It is only bread and wine, which we must live upon today."

"You speak the truth, perchance," said the soldier, "but if it is as you say, why does she turn away? Why does she not willingly let me see what she carries?"

"I do not wish that you shall see it," said the man, "and I command you to let us pass!"

With this he raised his axe, but the woman laid her hand on his arm.

"Enter not into strife!" she pleaded. "I will try some other way. I shall let him see what I bear, and I know that he can not harm it". With a proud and confident smile she turned toward the soldier, and threw back a fold of her robe.

Instantly the soldier staggered back and closed his eyes, as if dazed by a strong light. That which the woman held concealed under her robe reflected such a dazzling white light that at first he did not know what he saw.

"I thought you held a child on your arm," he said.

"You see what I hold," the woman answered.

Then the soldier finally saw that that which dazzled and shone was only a cluster of white lilies, the same kind that grew in the meadow; but their lustre was much richer and more radiant. He could hardly bear to look at them.

He stuck his hand in among the flowers. He couldn't help thinking that it must be a child the woman carried, but he felt only the cool flower-petals.

He was bitterly deceived, and in his wrath he would gladly have taken both the man and the woman prisoners, but he knew that he could give no reason for such a proceeding.

When the woman saw his confusion, she said: "Will you not let us go now?"

The soldier quietly lowered the spear and stepped aside.

The woman drew her robe over the flowers once more, and at the same time she looked with a sweet smile upon that which she bore on her arm. "I knew that you could not harm it, did you but see it," she said to the soldier.

50

With this, they hastened away; and the soldier stood and stared after them as long as they were within sight.

While he followed them with his eyes, he almost felt sure that the woman did not carry on her arm a cluster of lilies, but an actual, living child.

While he still stood and stared after the wanderers, he heard loud shouts from the street. It was Voltigius, with several of his men, who came running.

"Stop them!" they cried. "Close the gates on them! Don't let them escape!"

And when they came up to the soldier, they said that they had tracked the runaway boy. They had sought him in his home, but then he had escaped again. They had seen his parents hasten away with him. The father was a strong, grey-bearded man who carried an axe; the mother was a tall woman who held a child concealed under a raised robe.

At the same moment that Voltigius related this, there came a Bedouin riding in through the gate on a good horse. Without a word, the soldier rushed up to the rider, jerked him down off the horse and threw him to the ground, and, with one bound, jumped into the saddle and dashed away toward the road.

Two days later, the soldier rode forward through the dreary mountain-desert, which is the whole southern part of Judaea. All the while he was pursuing the three fugitives from Bethlehem, and he was beside himself because the fruitless hunt never came to an end.

"It looks, forsooth, as though these creatures had the power to sink into the earth," he grumbled. "How many times during these days have I not been so close to them that I've been on the point of throwing my spear at the child, and yet they have escaped me! I begin to think that I shall never catch up with them."

He felt despondent, like one who believes he is struggling against some superior power. He asked himself if it might not be possible that the gods protected these people against him.

"This trouble is in vain. Let me turn back before I perish from hunger and thirst in this barren land!" he said to himself, again and again. Then he was seized with fear of that which awaited him on his home-coming, should he turn back without having accomplished his mission.

Twice he had permitted the child to escape, and neither Voltigius nor Herod would pardon him for anything of the kind.

"As long as Herod knows that one of the Bethlehem children still lives, he will always be haunted by the same anxiety and dread," said the soldier. "Most likely he will try to ease his worries by nailing me to a cross."

It was a hot noonday hour, and he suffered tortures from the ride through this mountain district on a road which wound around steep cliffs where no breeze stirred. Both horse and rider were ready to drop.

Several hours before he had lost every trace of the fugitives, and he felt more disheartened than ever.

"I must give it up," thought he. "I verily believe it is time wasted to pursue them further. They must perish anyway in this awful wilderness."

As he thought this, he discovered, in a mountain-wall near the roadside, the vaulted entrance to a grotto.

Immediately he rode up to the opening. "I will rest a while in this cool mountain cave," thought he. "Then, mayhap, I can continue the pursuit with renewed strength."

As he was about to enter, he was struck with amazement! On each side of the opening grew a beautiful lily. The two stalks stood there tall and erect and full of blossoms. They sent forth an intoxicating odour of honey, and many bees buzzed around them.

It was such an uncommon sight in this wilderness that the soldier did something extraordinary. He broke off a large white flower and took it with him into the cave.

The cave was neither deep nor dark, and as soon as he entered he saw that there were already three travellers within: a man, a woman, and a child, who lay stretched out upon the ground, lost in deep slumber.

The soldier had never before felt his heart beat as it did at this vision. They were the three runaways whom he had hunted for so long. He recognized them instantly. And here they lay sleeping, unable to defend themselves and wholly in his power.

He drew his sword quickly and bent over the sleeping child.

Cautiously he lowered the sword toward the infant's heart, and measured carefully, in order to kill with a single thrust.

He paused an instant to look at the child's countenance. Now, when he was certain of victory, he felt a grim pleasure in beholding his victim.

But when he saw the child his joy increased, for he recognized the little boy whom he had seen play with the bees and lilies in the meadow beyond the city gate.

"Why, of course I should have understood this all the time!" thought he. "This is why I have always hated the child. This is the pretended Prince of Peace."

He lowered his sword again while he thought, "When I lay this child's head at Herod's feet he will make me Commander of his Life Guard."

As he brought the point of the sword nearer and nearer the heart of the sleeping child, he revelled in the thought: "This time, at least, no one shall come between us and snatch him from my power."

But the soldier still held in his hand the lily which he had broken off at the grotto entrance; and while he was thinking of his good fortune, a bee that had been hidden in its chalice flew towards him and buzzed around his head.

He staggered back. Suddenly he remembered the bees which the boy had carried to their home, and he remembered that it was a bee that had helped the child escape from Herod's feast. This thought struck him with surprise. He held the sword suspended, and stood still and listened for the bee.

Now he did not hear the tiny creature's buzzing. As he stood there, perfectly still, he became conscious of the strong, delicious

perfume which came from the lily that he held in his hand.

Then he began to think of the lilies that the little one had saved; he remembered that it was a cluster of lilies that had hidden the child from his view and made possible the escape through the city gate.

He became more and more thoughtful, and he drew back his sword.

"The bees and the lilies have requited his good deeds," he whispered to himself. Then he was struck by the thought that the little one had once shown even him a kindness, and a deep crimson flush mounted to his brow.

"Can a Roman soldier forget to requite an accepted service?" he whispered.

He fought a short battle with himself. He thought of Herod, and of his own desire to destroy the young Peace-Prince.

"It does not become me to murder this child who has saved my life," he said, at last.

And he bent down and laid his sword beside the child, that the fugitives on awakening should understand the danger they had escaped.

Then he saw that the child was awake. He lay and regarded the soldier with the beautiful eyes which shone like stars.

And the warrior bent a knee before the child.

"Lord, *thou* art the Mighty One!" said he. "Thou art the strong Conqueror! Thou art he whom the gods love! Thou art he who shall tread upon adders and scorpions!"

He kissed his feet and stole softly out from the grotto, while the little one smiled and smiled after him, with great, astonished child-eyes.

The Flight Into Egypt

Far away in one of the Eastern deserts many, many years ago grew a palm tree, which was both exceedingly old and exceedingly tall.

All who passed through the desert had to stop and gaze at it, for it was much larger than other palms; and they used to say of it, that some day it would certainly be taller than the obelisks and pyramids.

Where the huge palm tree stood in its solitude and looked out over the desert, it saw something one day which made its mighty leaf-crown sway back and forth on its slender trunk with astonishment. Over by the desert borders walked two human beings. They were still at the distance at which camels appear to be as tiny as moths; but they were certainly two human beings — two who were strangers in the desert; for the palm knew the desert-folk. They were a man and a woman who had neither guide nor pack-camels; neither tent nor water-sack.

"Verily," said the palm to itself, "These two have come hither only to meet certain death."

The palm cast a quick, apprehensive glance around.

"It surprises me," it said, "that the lions are not already out to hunt this prey, but I do not see a single one astir; nor do I see any of the desert robbers, but they'll probably soon come."

"A seven-fold death awaits these travellers," thought the palm. "The lions will devour them, thirst will parch them, the sand-storm will bury them, robbers will trap them, sunstroke will blight them, and fear will destroy them — " and the palm tried to think of

something else. The fate of these people made it sad at heart.

But on the whole desert plain, which lay spread out beneath the palm, there was nothing which it had not known and looked upon these thousand years. Nothing in particular could arrest its attention. Again it had to think of the two wanderers.

"By the drought and the storm!" said the palm, calling upon Life's most dangerous enemies. "What is that that the woman carries on her arm? I believe these fools also bring a little child with them!"

The palm, who was far-sighted — as the old usually are — actually saw aright. The woman bore on her arm a child, that leaned against her shoulder and slept.

"The child hasn't even sufficient clothing on," said the palm. "I see that the mother has tucked up her skirt and thrown it over the child. She must have snatched him from his bed in great haste and rushed off with him. I understand now: these people are runaways.

"But they are fools, nevertheless," continued the palm. "Unless an angel protects them, they would have done better to have let their enemies do their worst, than to venture into this wilderness.

"I can imagine how the whole thing came about. The man stood at his work; the child slept in his crib; the woman had gone out to fetch water. When she was a few steps from the door, she saw enemies coming. She rushed back to the house, snatched up her child, and fled.

"Since then, they have been fleeing for several days. It is very certain that they have not rested a moment. Yes, everything has happened in this way, but still I say that unless an angel protects them —

"They are so frightened that, as yet, they feel neither fatigue nor suffering. But I see their thirst by the strange gleam in their eyes. Surely I ought to know a thirsty person's face!"

And when the palm began to think of thirst, a shudder passed through its tall trunk, and the long leaves' numberless lobes rolled up, as though they had been held over a fire.

"Were I a human being," it said, "I should never venture into the desert. He is pretty brave who dares come here without having roots that reach down to the never-dying water veins. Here it can be dangerous even for palms; yes, even for a palm such as I.

"If I could counsel them, I should beg them to turn back. Their enemies could never be as cruel toward them as the desert. Perhaps they think it is easy to live in the desert! But I know that, now and then, even I have found it hard to keep alive. I recollect one time in my youth when a hurricane threw a whole mountain of sand over me. I came near choking. If I could have died that would have been my last moment."

The palm continued to think aloud, as the aged and solitary habitually do.

"I hear a wondrously beautiful melody rush through my leaves," it said. "All the lobes on my leaves are quivering. I know not what it is that takes possession of me at the sight of these poor strangers. But this unfortunate woman is so beautiful! She carries me back, in memory, to the most wonderful thing that I ever experienced."

And while the leaves continued to move in a soft melody, the palm was reminded how once, very long ago, two illustrious personages had visited the oasis. They were the Queen of Sheba and Solomon the Wise. The beautiful Queen was to return to her own country; the King had accompanied her on the journey, and now they were going to part. "In remembrance of this hour," said the Queen then, "I now plant a date seed in the earth, and I wish that from it shall spring a palm which shall grow and live until a King shall arise in Judaea, greater than Solomon." And when she had said this, she planted the seed in the earth and watered it with her tears.

"How does it happen that I am thinking of this just today?" said the palm. "Can this woman be so beautiful that she reminds me of the most glorious of queens, of her by whose word I have lived and flourished until this day?

"I hear my leaves rustle louder and louder," said the palm, "and it sounds as melancholy as a dirge. It is as though they prophesied that some one would soon leave this life. It is well to know that it does not apply to me, since I cannot die."

The palm assumed that the death-rustle in its leaves must apply to the two lone wanderers. It is certain that they too believed that their last hour was nearing. One saw it from their expression as they walked past the skeleton of a camel which lay in their path. One saw it from the glances they cast back at a pair of passing vultures. It couldn't be otherwise; they must perish!

They had caught sight of the palm and oasis and hastened thither to find water. But when they arrived at last, they collapsed from despair, for the well was dry. The woman, worn out, laid the child down and seated herself beside the well-curb, and wept. The man flung himself down beside her and beat upon the dry earth with his fists. The palm heard how they talked with each other about their inevitable death. It also gleaned from their conversation that King Herod had ordered the slaughter of all male children from two to three years old, because he feared that the long-looked-for King of the Jews had been born.

"It rustles louder and louder in my leaves," said the palm. "These poor fugitives will soon see their last moment."

It perceived also that they dreaded the desert. The man said it would have been better if they had stayed at home and fought with the soldiers, than to fly hither. He said that they would have met an easier death.

"God will help us," said the woman.

"We are alone among beasts of prey and serpents," said the man. "We have no food and no water. How should God be able to help us?" In despair he rent his garments and pressed his face against the dry earth. He was without hope — like a man with a death-wound in his heart.

The woman sat erect, with her hands clasped over her knees. But the looks she cast toward the desert spoke of a hopelessness beyond bounds.

The palm heard the melancholy rustle in its leaves growing louder and louder. The woman must have heard it also, for she turned her gaze upward toward the palm-crowns. And instantly she involuntarily raised her arms.

"Oh, dates, dates!" she cried. There was such intense agony in her voice that the old palm wished itself no taller than a broom and that the dates were as easy to reach as the buds on a briar bush. It probably knew that its crown was full of date clusters, but how should a human being reach such a height?

The man had already seen how beyond all reach the date clusters

hung. He did not even raise his head. He begged his wife not to long for the impossible.

But the child, who had toddled about by himself and played with sticks and straws, had heard the mother's outcry.

Of course the little one could not imagine that his mother should not get everything she wished for. The instant she said dates, he began to stare at the tree. He pondered and pondered how he should bring down the dates. His forehead was almost drawn into wrinkles under the golden curls. At last a smile stole over his face. He had found the way. He went up to the palm and stroked it with his little hand, and said, in a sweet, childish voice:

"Palm, bend thyself! Palm, bend thyself!"

But what was that, what was that? The palm leaves rustled as if a hurricane had passed through them, and up and down the long trunk travelled shudder upon shudder. And the tree felt that the little one was its superior. It could not resist him.

And it bowed its long trunk before the child, as people bow before princes. In a great bow it bent itself toward the ground, and finally it came down so far that the big crown with the trembling leaves swept the desert sand.

The child appeared to be neither frightened nor surprised; with a joyous cry he loosened cluster after cluster from the old palm's crown. When he had plucked enough dates, and the tree still lay on the ground, the child came back again and caressed it and said, in the gentlest voice:

"Palm, raise thyself! Palm, raise thyself!"

Slowly and reverently the big tree raised itself on its slender trunk, while the leaves played like harps.

"Now I know for whom they are playing the death melody," said the palm to itself when it stood erect once more. "It is not for any of these people."

The man and the woman sank upon their knees and thanked God.

"Thou hast seen our agony and removed it. Thou art the Powerful One who bendest the palm-trunk like a reed. What enemy should we fear when Thy strength protects us?"

The next time a caravan passed through the desert, the travellers saw that the great palm's leaf-crown had withered.

"How can this be?" said a traveller. "This palm was not to die before it had seen a King greater than Solomon."

"Mayhap it has seen him," answered another of the desert travellers.

In Nazareth

Once, when Jesus was only five years old, he sat on the doorstep outside his father's workshop, in Nazareth, and made clay cuckoos from a lump of clay which the potter across the way had given him.

He was happier than usual. All the children in the quarter had told Jesus that the potter was a disobliging man, who wouldn't let himself be coaxed, either by soft glances or honeyed words, and he had never dared ask aught of him. But, you see, he hardly knew how it had come about. He had only stood on his doorstep and, with yearning eyes, looked upon the neighbour working at his moulds, and then that neighbour had come over from his stall and given him so much clay that it would have been enough to finish a whole wine jug.

On the stoop of the next house sat Judas, his face covered with bruises and his clothes full of rents, which he had acquired during his continual fights with street urchins. For the moment he was quiet, he neither quarrelled nor fought, but worked with a bit of clay, just as Jesus did. But this clay he had not been able to procure for himself. He hardly dared venture within sight of the potter, who complained that he was in the habit of throwing stones at his fragile wares, and would have driven him away with a good beating. It was Jesus who had divided his portion with him.

When the two children had finished their clay cuckoos, they stood the birds up in a ring in front of them. These looked just as clay cuckoos have always looked. They had big, round lumps to stand on in place of feet, short tails, no necks, and almost imperceptible wings.

But, at all events, one saw at once a difference in the work of the little playmates. Judas's birds were so crooked that they tumbled over continually; and no matter how hard he worked with his clumsy little fingers, he couldn't get their bodies neat and well formed. Now and then he glanced slyly at Jesus, to see how he managed to make his birds as smooth and even as the oak-leaves in the forests on Mount Tabor.

As bird after bird was finished, Jesus became happier and happier. Each looked more beautiful to him than the last, and he regarded them all with pride and affection. They were to be his playmates, his little brothers; they should sleep in his bed, keep him company, and sing to him when his mother left him. Never before had he thought himself so rich; never again could he feel alone or forsaken.

The big brawny water-carrier came walking along, and right after him came the huckster, who sat joggingly on his donkey between the large empty willow baskets. The water-carrier laid his hand on Jesus's curly head and asked him about his birds; and Jesus told him that they had names and that they could sing. All the little birds had come to him from foreign lands, and told him things which only he and they knew. And Jesus spoke in such a way that both the water-carrier and the huckster forgot about their tasks for a full hour, to listen to him.

But when they wished to go farther, Jesus pointed to Judas. "See what pretty birds Judas makes!" he said.

Then the huckster good-naturedly stopped his donkey and asked Judas if his birds also had names and could sing. But Judas knew nothing of this. He was stubbornly silent and did not raise his eyes from his work, and the huckster angrily kicked one of his birds and rode on.

In this manner the afternoon passed, and the sun sank so far down that its beams could come in through the low city gate, which stood at the end of the street and was decorated with a Roman Eagle. This sunshine, which came at the close of the day, was perfectly rose-red — as if it had become mixed with blood — and it coloured everything which came in its path, as it filtered through the narrow street. It painted the potter's vessels as well as the log which creaked under the woodman's saw, and the white veil that covered Mary's face.

But the loveliest of all was the sun's reflection as it shone on the little water-puddles which had gathered in the big, uneven cracks in the stones that covered the street. Suddenly Jesus stuck his hand in the puddle nearest him. He had conceived the idea that he would paint his grey birds with the sparkling sunbeams which had given such pretty colour to the water, the house-walls, and everything around him.

The sunshine took pleasure in letting itself be captured by him, like paint in a paint pot; and when Jesus spread it over the little clay birds, it lay still and bedecked them from head to feet with a diamond-like lustre.

Judas, who every now and then looked at Jesus to see if he made more and prettier birds than his, gave a shriek of delight when he saw how Jesus painted his clay cuckoos with the sunshine, which he caught from the water pools. Judas also dipped his hand in the shining water and tried to catch the sunshine.

But the sunshine wouldn't be caught by him. It slipped through his fingers; and no matter how fast he tried to move his hands to get hold of it, it got away, and he couldn't procure a pinch of colour for his poor birds.

"Wait, Judas!" said Jesus. "I'll come and paint your birds."

"No, you shan't touch them!" cried Judas. "They're good enough as they are."

He rose, his eyebrows contracted into an ugly frown, his lips compressed. And he put his broad foot on the birds and transformed them, one after another, into little flat pieces of clay.

When all his birds were destroyed, he walked over to Jesus, who sat and caressed his birds that glittered like jewels. Judas regarded them for a moment in silence, then he raised his foot and crushed one of them.

When Judas took his foot away and saw the entire little bird changed into a cake of clay, he felt so relieved that he began to laugh, and raised his foot to crush another.

"Judas," said Jesus, "what are you doing? Don't you see that they are alive and can sing?"

But Judas laughed and crushed still another bird.

Jesus looked around for help. Judas was heavily built and Jesus had not the strength to hold him back. He glanced around for his

mother. She was not far away, but before she could have got there, Judas would have had ample time to destroy the birds. The tears sprang to Jesus's eyes. Judas had already crushed four of his birds. There were only three left.

He was annoyed with his birds, who stood so calmly and let themselves be trampled upon without paying the slightest attention to the danger. Jesus clapped his hands to awaken them; then he shouted: "Fly, fly!"

Then the three birds began to move their tiny wings, and, fluttering anxiously, they succeeded in swinging themselves up to the eaves of the house, where they were safe.

But when Judas saw that the birds took to their wings and flew at Jesus's command, he began to weep. He tore his hair, as he had seen his elders do when they were in great trouble, and he threw himself at Jesus's feet.

Judas lay there and rolled in the dust before Jesus like a dog, and kissed his feet and begged that he would raise his foot and crush him, as he had done with the clay cuckoos. For Judas loved Jesus and admired and worshipped him, and at the same time hated him.

Mary, who sat all the while and watched the children's play, came up and lifted Judas in her arms and seated him on her lap, and caressed him.

"You poor child!" she said to him, "you do not know that you have attempted something which no mortal can accomplish. Don't engage in anything of this kind again, if you do not wish to become the unhappiest of mortals! What would happen to any one of us who undertook to compete with one who paints with sunbeams and blows the breath of life into dead clay?"

In the Temple

Once there was a poor family — a man, his wife, and their little son — who walked about in the big Temple at Jerusalem. The son was such a pretty child! He had hair which fell in long, even curls, and eyes that shone like stars.

The son had not been in the Temple since he was big enough to comprehend what he saw; and now his parents showed him all its glories. There were long rows of pillars and gilded altars; there were holy men who sat and instructed their pupils; there was the high priest with his breastplate of precious stones. There were the curtains from Babylon, interwoven with gold roses; there were the great copper gates, which were so heavy that it was hard work for thirty men to swing them back and forth on their hinges.

But the little boy, who was only twelve years old, did not care very much about seeing all this. His mother told him that what she showed him was the most marvellous in all the world. She told him that it would probably be a long time before he should see anything like it again. In the poor town of Nazareth, where they lived, there was nothing to be seen but grey streets.

Her exhortations did not help matters much. The little boy looked as though he would willingly have run away from the magnificent Temple, if instead he could have got out and played on the narrow street in Nazareth.

But it was singular that the more indifferent the boy appeared, the

71

more pleased and happy were the parents. They nodded to each other over his head, and were thoroughly satisfied.

At last, the little one looked so tired and bored that the mother felt sorry for him. "Now we have walked too far with you," said she. "Come, you shall rest awhile."

She sat down beside a pillar and told him to lie down on the ground and rest his head on her knee. He did so, and fell asleep instantly.

He had barely closed his eyes when the wife said to the husband: "I have never feared anything so much as the moment when he should come here to Jerusalem's Temple. I believed that when he saw this house of God, he would wish to stay here for ever."

"I, too, have been afraid of this journey," said the man. "At the time of his birth, many signs and wonders appeared which betokened that he would become a great ruler. But what could royal honours bring him except worries and dangers? I have always said that it would be best, both for him and for us, if he never became anything but a carpenter in Nazareth."

"Since his fifth year," said the mother reflectively, "no miracles have happened around him. And he does not recall any of the wonders which occurred during his early childhood. Now he is exactly like a child among other children. God's will be done above all else! But I have almost begun to hope that Our Lord in His mercy will choose another for the great destinies, and let me keep my son with me."

"For my part," said the man, "I am certain that if he learns nothing of the signs and wonders which occurred during his first years, then all will go well."

"I never speak with him about any of these marvels," said the wife. "But I fear all the while that, without my having aught to do with it, something will happen which will make him understand who he is. I feared most of all to bring him to this Temple."

"You may be glad that the danger is over now," said the man. "We shall soon have him back home in Nazareth."

"I have feared the wise men in the Temple," said the woman. "I have dreaded the soothsayers who sit here on their rugs. I believed that when he should come to their notice, they would stand up and bow before the child, and greet him as Judaea's King. It is singular that they do not notice his beauty. Such a child has never before come under their eyes." She sat in silence a moment and regarded the child. "I can hardly understand it," said she. "I believed that when he should see these judges, who sit in the house of the Holy One and settle the people's disputes, and these teachers who talk with their pupils, and these priests who serve the Lord, he would wake up and say: 'It is here, among these judges, these teachers, these priests, that I am born to live'."

"What happiness would there be for him to sit shut in between these pillar-aisles?" interposed the man. "It is better for him to roam on the hills and mountains round about Nazareth."

The mother sighed a little. "He is so happy at home with us!" said she. "How contented he seems when he can follow the shepherds on their lonely wanderings, or when he can go out in the fields and see the husbandmen labour. I cannot believe that we are treating him wrongly, when we seek to keep him for ourselves."

"We only spare him the greatest suffering," said the man.

They continued talking together in this strain until the child awoke from his slumber.

"Well," said the mother, "have you had a good rest? Stand up now, for it is drawing on toward evening, and we must return to the camp."

They were in the most remote part of the building and so began the walk towards the entrance.

They had to go through an old arch which had been there ever since the time when the first Temple was erected on this spot; and near the arch, propped against a wall, stood an old copper trumpet, enormous in length and weight, almost like a pillar to raise to the mouth and play upon. It stood there dented and battered, full of dust and spiders' webs, inside and outside, and covered with an almost invisible tracing of ancient letters. Probably a thousand years had gone by since anyone had tried to coax a tone out of it.

But when the little boy saw the huge trumpet, he stopped — astonished! "What is that?" he asked.

"That is the great trumpet called the Voice of the Prince of this World," replied the mother. "With this, Moses called together the Children of Israel, when they were scattered over the wilderness. Since his time no one has been able to coax a single tone from it. But he who can do this, shall gather all the peoples of earth under his dominion."

She smiled at this, which she believed to be an old myth; but the little boy remained standing beside the big trumpet until she called him. This trumpet was the first thing he had seen in the Temple that he liked.

They had not gone far before they came to a big, wide Temple-court. Here, in the mountain-foundation itself, was a chasm, deep and wide — just as it had been from time immemorial. This chasm King Solomon had not wished to fill in when he built the Temple. No bridge had been laid over it; no enclosure had he built around the steep abyss. But instead, he had stretched across it a sword of steel, several feet long, sharpened, and with the blade up. And after ages and ages and many changes, the sword still lay across the chasm. Now it had almost rusted away. It was no longer securely fastened at the ends, but trembled and rocked as soon as anyone walked with heavy steps in the Temple Court.

When the mother took the boy in a roundabout way past the chasm, he asked: "What bridge is this?"

"It was placed there by King Solomon," answered the mother, "and we call it Paradise Bridge. If you can cross the chasm on this trembling bridge, whose surface is thinner than a sunbeam, then you can be sure of getting to Paradise."

She smiled and moved away; but the boy stood still and looked at the narrow, trembling steel blade until she called him.

When he obeyed her, she sighed because she had not shown him these two remarkable things sooner, so that he might have had sufficient time to view them.

Now they walked on without being detained, till they came to the great entrance portico with its columns, five-deep. Here, in a corner, were two black marble pillars erected on the same foundation, and so close to each other that hardly a straw could be squeezed in between them. They were tall and majestic, with richly ornamented capitals around which ran a row of peculiarly formed beasts' heads. And there was not an inch on these beautiful pillars that did not bear marks and scratches. They were worn and damaged like nothing else in the Temple. Even the floor around them was worn smooth, and was somewhat hollowed out from the wear of many feet.

Once more the boy stopped his mother and asked: "What pillars are these?"

"They are pillars which our father Abraham brought with him to Palestine from far-away Chaldea, and which he called Righteousness' Gate. He who can squeeze between them is righteous before God and has never committed a sin."

The boy stood still and regarded these pillars with great, open eyes.

"You, surely, do not think of trying to squeeze yourself in between them?" laughed the mother. "You see how the floor around them is worn away by the many who have attempted to force their way through the narrow space; but, believe me, no one has succeeded. Make haste! I hear the clanging of the copper gates; the thirty Temple servants have put their shoulders to them.''

But all night the little boy lay awake in the tent, and he saw before him nothing but Righteousness' Gate and Paradise Bridge and the Voice of the Prince of this World. Never before had he heard of such wonderful things, and he couldn't get them out of his head.

And on the morning of the next day it was the same thing: he couldn't think of anything else. That morning they were to leave for home. The parents had much to do before they took the tent down and loaded it upon a big camel, and before everything else was in order. They were not going to travel alone, but in company with many relatives and neighbours. And since there were so many, the packing naturally went on very slowly.

The little boy did not assist in the work, but in the midst of the hurry and confusion he sat still and thought about the three wonderful things.

Suddenly he concluded that he would have time enough to go back to the Temple and take another look at them. There was still much to be packed away. He could probably manage to get back from the Temple before the departure.

He hastened away without telling anyone where he was going to. He didn't think it was necessary. He would soon return, of course.

It wasn't long before he reached the Temple and entered the portico where the two pillars stood.

As soon as he saw them, his eyes danced with joy. He sat down on the floor beside them, and gazed up at them. As he thought that he who could squeeze between these two pillars was accounted righteous before God and had never committed sin, he fancied he had never seen anything so wonderful.

He thought how glorious it would be to be able to squeeze in between the two pillars, but they stood so close together that it was impossible even to try it. In this way, he sat motionless before the pillars for well-nigh an hour; but this he did not know. He thought he had looked at them only a few moments.

But it happened that, in the portico where the little boy sat, the judges of the high court were assembled to help folks settle their differences.

The whole portico was filled with people who complained about boundary lines that had been moved, about sheep which had been carried away from the flocks and branded with false marks, about debtors who wouldn't pay.

Among them came a rich man dressed in a trailing purple robe, who brought before the court a poor widow who was supposed to owe him a few silver shekels. The poor widow cried and said that the rich man dealt unjustly with her; she had already paid her debt to him once, and now he tried to force her to pay it again, but this she could not afford to do; she was so poor that should the judges condemn her to pay, she must give her daughters to the rich man as slaves.

Then he who sat in the place of honour on the judges' bench, turned to the rich man and said: "Do you dare to swear on oath that this poor woman has not already paid you?"

Then the rich man answered: "Lord, I am a rich man. Would I take the trouble to demand my money from this poor widow, if I did not have the right to it? I swear to you that as certain as that no one shall ever walk through Righteousness' Gate does this woman owe me the sum which I demand."

When the judges heard this oath they believed him, and doomed the poor widow to leave him her daughters as slaves.

But the little boy sat close by and heard all this. He thought to himself: What a good thing it would be if someone could squeeze through Righteousness' Gate! That rich man certainly did not speak the truth. It is a great pity about the poor old woman, who will be compelled to send her daughters away to become slaves!

He jumped upon the platform where the two pillars towered into the heights, and looked through the crack.

"Ah, that it were not altogether impossible!" thought he.

He was deeply distressed because of the poor woman. Now he didn't think at all about the saying that he who could squeeze through Righteousness' Gate was holy, and without sin. He wanted to get through only for the sake of the poor woman.

He put his shoulder in the groove between the two pillars, as if to make a way.

That instant all the people who stood under the portico, looked over toward Righteousness' Gate. For it rumbled in the vaults, and it sang in the old pillars, and they glided apart — one to the right, and one to the left — and made a space wide enough for the boy's slender body to pass between them!

Then there arose the greatest wonder and excitement! At first no one knew what to say. The people stood and stared at the little boy who had worked so great a miracle.

The oldest among the judges was the first one who came to his senses. He called out that they should lay hold on the rich merchant, and bring him before the judgment seat. And he sentenced him to leave all his goods to the poor widow, because he had sworn falsely in God's Temple.

When this was settled, the judge asked after the boy who had passed through Righteousness' Gate; but when the people looked around for him, he had disappeared. For the very moment the pillars glided apart, he was awakened, as from a dream, and remembered the home-journey and his parents. "Now I must hasten away from here, so that my parents will not have to wait for me," thought he.

He knew not that he had sat a whole hour before Righteousness' Gate, but believed he had lingered there only a few minutes; therefore, he thought that he would even have time to take a look at Paradise Bridge before he left the Temple.

And he slipped through the throng of people and came to Paradise Bridge, which was situated in another part of the big temple.

But when he saw the sharp steel sword which was drawn across the chasm, he though how the person who could walk across that bridge was sure of reaching Paradise. He believed that this was the most marvellous thing he had ever beheld; and he seated himself on the edge of the chasm to look at the steel sword.

There he sat down and thought how delightful it would be to reach Paradise, and how much he would like to walk across the bridge; but at the same time he saw that it would be simply impossible even to attempt it.

Thus he sat and mused for two hours, but he did not know how the time had flown. He sat there and thought only of Paradise.

But it seems that in the court where the deep chasm was, a large altar had been erected, and all around it walked white-robed priests, who tended the altar fire and received sacrifices. In the court there were many with offerings, and a big crowd who only watched the service.

Then there came a poor old man who brought a lamb which was very small and thin, and which had been bitten by a dog and had a large wound.

The man went up to the priests with the lamb and begged that he might offer it, but they refused to accept it. They told him that such a miserable gift he could not offer to Our Lord. The old man implored them to accept the lamb out of compassion, for his son lay at the point of death, and he possessed nothing else that he could offer to

God for his restoration. "You must let me offer it," said he, "else my prayers will not come before God's face and my son will die!"

"You must not believe but that I have the greatest sympathy with you," said the priest, "but in the law it is forbidden to sacrifice a damaged animal. It is just as impossible to grant your prayers, as it is to cross Paradise Bridge."

The little boy did not sit very far away, so he heard all this. Instantly he thought what a pity it was that no one could cross the bridge. Perhaps the poor man might keep his son if the lamb were sacrificed.

The old man left the Temple Court disconsolate, but the boy got up, walked over to the trembling bridge, and put his foot on it.

He didn't think at all about wanting to cross it to be certain of Paradise. His thoughts were with the poor man, whom he desired to help.

But he drew back his foot, for he thought: "This is impossible. It is much too old and rusty, and would not hold even me!"

But once again his thoughts went out to the old man whose son lay at death's door. Again he put his foot down upon the blade.

Then he noticed that it ceased to tremble, and that beneath his foot it felt broad and secure.

And when he took the next step upon it, he felt that the air around him supported him, so that he could not fall. It bore him as though he were a bird, and had wings.

But from the suspended sword a sweet tone trembled when the boy walked upon it, and one of those who stood in the court turned around when he heard the tone. He gave a cry, and then the others turned and saw the little boy tripping across the sword.

There was great consternation among all who stood there. The first who came to their senses were the priests. They immediately sent a messenger after the poor man, and when he came back they said to him: "God has performed a miracle to show us that He will accept your offering. Give us your lamb and we will sacrifice it."

When this was done they asked for the little boy who had walked across the chasm; but when they looked around for him they could not find him.

For just after the boy had crossed the chasm, he happened to think of the journey home, and of his parents. He did not know that the morning and the whole forenoon were gone, but thought: "I must make haste and get back, so that they will not have to wait. But first I want to run over and take a look at the Voice of the Prince of this World."

And he stole away through the crowd and ran over to the damp pillar-aisle where the copper trumpet stood leaning against the wall.

When he saw it, and thought about the prediction that he who could coax a tone from it should one day gather all the peoples of earth under his dominion, he fancied that never had he seen anything so wonderful! and he sat down beside it and regarded it.

He thought how great it would be to win all the peoples of earth, and how much he wished that he could blow in the old trumpet. But he understood that it was impossible, so he didn't even dare try.

He sat like this for several hours, but he did not know how the time passed. He thought only how marvellous it would be to gather all the peoples of earth under his dominion.

But it happened that in this cool passage sat a holy man who instructed his pupils, that sat at his feet.

And now this holy man turned toward one of his pupils and told him that he was an impostor. He said the spirit had revealed to him that this youth was a stranger, and not an Israelite. And he demanded why he had sneaked in among his pupils under a false name.

Then the strange youth rose and said that he had wandered through deserts and sailed over great seas that he might hear wisdom and the doctrine of the only true God expounded. "My soul was faint with longing," he said to the holy man. "But I knew that you would not teach me if I did not say that I was an Israelite. Therefore, I lied to you, that my longing should be satisfied. And I pray that you will let me remain here with you."

But the holy man stood up and raised his arms toward heaven. "It is just as impossible to let you remain here with me, as it is that some one shall arise and blow in the huge copper trumpet, which we call the Voice of the Prince of this World! You are not even permitted to enter this part of the Temple. Leave this place at once, or my pupils will throw themselves upon you and tear you in pieces, for your presence desecrates the Temple."

But the youth stood still, and said: "I do not wish to go elsewhere, where my soul can find no nourishment. I would rather die here at your feet."

Hardly was this said when the holy man's pupils jumped to their feet, to drive him away, and when he made resistance, they threw him down and wished to kill him.

But the boy sat very near, so he heard and saw all this, and he thought: "This is a great injustice. Oh, if I could only blow in the big copper trumpet, he would be helped."

He rose and laid his hand on the trumpet. At this moment he no longer wished that he could raise it to his lips because he who could do so should be a great ruler, but because he hoped that he might help one whose life was in danger.

And he grasped the copper trumpet with his tiny hands, to try and lift it.

Then he felt that the huge trumpet raised itself to his lips. And when he only breathed, a strong, resonant tone came forth from the trumpet, and reverberated all through the great Temple.

Then they all turned their eyes and saw that it was a little boy who stood with the trumpet to his lips and coaxed from it tones which made foundations and pillars tremble.

Instantly, all the hands which had been lifted to strike the strange youth fell, and the holy teacher said to him:

"Come and sit thee here at my feet, as thou didst sit before! God hath performed a miracle to show me that it is His wish that thou shouldst be consecrated to His service."

As it drew on toward the close of day, a man and a woman came hurrying toward Jerusalem. They looked frightened and anxious, and called out to each and every one whom they met: "We have lost our son! We thought he had followed our relatives, but none of them have seen him. Has any one of you passed a child alone?"

Those who came from Jerusalem answered them: "Indeed, we have not seen your son, but in the Temple we saw a most beautiful child! He was like an angel from heaven, and he has passed through Righteousness' Gate."

They would gladly have related, very minutely, all about this, but the parents had no time to listen.

When they had walked on a little farther, they met other persons and questioned them.

But those who came from Jerusalem wished to talk only about a most beautiful child who looked as though he had come down from heaven, and who had crossed Paradise Bridge.

They would gladly have stopped and talked about this until late at night, but the man and woman had no time to listen to them, and hurried into the city.

They walked up one street and down another without finding the child. At last they reached the Temple. As they came up to it, the woman said: "Since we are here, let us go in and see what the child is like, which they say has come down from heaven!" They went in and asked where they should find the child.

"Go straight on to where the holy teachers sit with their students. There you will find the child. The old men have seated him in their midst. They question him and he questions them, and they are all amazed at him. But all the people stand below in the Temple court, to catch a glimpse of the one who has raised the Voice of the Prince of this World to his lips."

The man and the woman made their way through the throng of

people, and saw that the child who sat among the wise teachers was their son.

But as soon as the woman recognized the child she began to weep.

And the boy who sat among the wise men heard that someone wept, and he knew that it was his mother. Then he rose and came over to her, and the father and mother took him between them and went from the Temple with him.

But as the mother continued to weep, the child asked: "Why weepest thou? I came to thee as soon as I heard thy voice."

"Should I not weep?" said the mother. "I believed that thou wert lost to me."

They went out from the city and darkness came on, and all the while the mother wept.

"Why weepest thou?" asked the child. "I did not know that the day was spent. I thought it was still morning, and I came to thee as soon as I heard thy voice."

"Should I not weep?" said the mother. "I have sought for thee all day long. I believed that thou wert lost to me."

They walked the whole night, and the mother wept all the while.

When day began to dawn, the child said: "Why dost thou weep? I have not sought mine own glory, but God has let me perform miracles because He wanted to help the three poor creatures. As soon as I heard thy voice, I came to thee."

"My son," replied the mother. "I weep because thou art none the less lost to me. Thou wilt never more belong to me. Henceforth thy life ambition shall be righteousness; thy longing, Paradise; and thy love shall embrace all the poor human beings who people this earth."

Saint Veronica

I

During one of the latter years of Emperor Tiberius's reign, a poor vine-dresser and his wife came and settled in a solitary hut among the Sabine mountains. They were strangers, and lived in absolute solitude without ever receiving a visit from a human being. But one morning when the labourer opened his door, he found, to his astonishment, that an old woman sat huddled up on the threshold.

She was wrapped in a plain grey mantle, and looked very poor. Nevertheless, she impressed him as being so respect-compelling, as she rose and came to meet him, that it made him think of what the legends had to say about goddesses who, in the form of old women, had visited mortals.

"My friend," said the old woman to the vine-dresser, "you must not wonder that I have slept this night on your threshold. My parents lived in this hut, and here I was born nearly ninety years ago. I expected to find it empty and deserted. I did not know that people still occupied it."

"I do not wonder that you thought a hut which lies so high up among these desolate hills should stand empty and deserted," said the vine-dresser. "But my wife and I come from a foreign land, and as poor strangers we have not been able to find a better dwelling-place. But to you, who must be tired and hungry after the long journey, which you at your extreme age have undertaken, it is perhaps more welcome that the hut is occupied by people than by Sabine mountain wolves. You will at least find a bed within to rest on, and a bowl of goat's milk, and a bread-cake, if you will accept them."

The old woman smiled a little, but this smile was so fleeting that it could not dispel the expression of deep sorrow which rested upon her countenance.

"I spent my entire youth up here among these mountains," she said. "I have not yet forgotten the trick of driving a wolf from his lair."

And she actually looked so strong and vigorous that the labourer didn't doubt that she still possessed strength enough, despite her great age, to fight with the wild beasts of the forest.

He repeated his invitation, and the old woman stepped into the cottage. She sat down to the frugal meal, and partook of it without hesitancy. Although she seemed to be well satisfied with the fare of coarse bread soaked in goat's milk, both the man and his wife thought: "Where can this old wanderer come from? She has certainly eaten pheasants served on silver plates oftener than she has drunk goat's milk from earthen bowls."

Now and then she raised her eyes from the food and looked around, — as if to try and realize that she was back in the hut. The poor old home with its bare clay walls and its earth floor was certainly not much changed. She pointed out to her hosts that on the walls there were still visible some traces of dogs and deer which her father had sketched there to amuse his little children. And on a shelf, high up, she thought she saw fragments of an earthen dish which she herself had used to measure milk in.

The man and his wife thought to themselves: "It must be true that she was born in this hut, but she has surely had much more to attend to in this life than milking goats and making butter and cheese."

They observed also that her thoughts were often far away, and that she sighed heavily and anxiously every time she came back to herself.

Finally she rose from the table. She thanked them graciously for the hospitality she had enjoyed, and walked toward the door.

But then it seemd to the vine-dresser that she was pitifully poor and lonely, and he exclaimed: "If I am not mistaken, it was not your intention when you dragged yourself up here last night, to leave this hut so soon. If you are actually as poor as you seem, it must have been your intention to remain here for the rest of your life. But now you wish to leave because my wife and I have taken possession of the hut."

The old woman did not deny that he had guessed rightly. "But this hut, which for many years has been deserted, belongs to you as much as to me," she said. "I have no right to drive you from it."

"It is still your parents' hut," said the labourer, "and you surely have a better right to it than we have. Besides, we are young and you are old; therefore, you shall remain and we will go."

When the old woman heard this, she was greatly astonished. She turned around on the threshold and stared at the man, as though she had not understood what he meant by his words.

But now the young wife joined in the conversation.

"If I might suggest," said she to her husband, "I should beg you to ask this old woman if she won't look upon us as her own children, and permit us to stay with her and take care of her. What service would we render her if we gave her this miserable hut and then left her? It would be terrible for her to live here in this wilderness alone! And what would she live on? It would be just like letting her starve to death."

The old woman went up to the man and his wife and regarded them carefully. "Why do you speak thus?" she asked. "Why are you so merciful to me? You are strangers."

Then the young wife answered: "It is because we ourselves once met with great mercy."

II

This is how the old woman came to live in the vine-dresser's hut. And she conceived a great friendship for the young people. But for all that she never told them whence she had come, or who she was, and they understood that she would not have taken it in good part had they questioned her.

But one evening, when the day's work was done, and all three sat on the big, flat rock which lay before the entrance, and partook of their evening meal, they saw an old man coming up the path.

He was a tall and powerfully built man, with shoulders as broad as a gladiator's. His face wore a cheerless and stern expression. The brows jutted far out over the deep-set eyes, and the lines around the mouth expressed bitterness and contempt. He walked with erect bearing and quick movements.

The man wore a simple dress, and the instant the vine-dresser saw him, he said: "He is an old soldier, one who has been discharged from service and is now on his way home."

When the stranger came direcly before them he paused, as if in doubt. The labourer, who knew that the road terminated a short distance beyond the hut, laid down his spoon and called out to him: "Have you gone astray, stranger, since you come hither? Usually, no one takes the trouble to climb up here, unless he has an errand to one of us who live here."

When he questioned in this manner, the stranger came nearer. "It is as you say," said he. "I have taken the wrong road, and now I know not whither I shall direct my steps. If you will let me rest here a while, and then tell me which path I shall follow to get to some farm, I shall be grateful to you."

As he spake he sat down upon one of the stones which lay before the hut. The young woman asked him if he wouldn't share their supper, but this he declined with a smile. On the other hand it was very evident that he was inclined to talk with them, while they ate. He asked the young folks about their manner of living, and their work, and they answered him frankly and cheerfully.

Suddenly the labourer turned toward the stranger and began to question him. "You see in what a lonely and isolated way we live," said he. "It must be a year at least since I have talked with any one except shepherds and vineyard labourers. Can not you, who must come from some camp, tell us something about Rome and the Emperor?"

Hardly had the man said this than the young wife noticed that the old woman gave him a warning glance, and made with her hand the sign which means — Have a care what you say.

The stranger, meanwhile, answered very affably: "I understand that you take me for a soldier, which is not untrue, although I have long since left the service. During Tiberius's reign there has not been much work for us soldiers. Yet he was once a great commander. Those were the days of his good fortune. Now he thinks of nothing except to guard himself against conspiracies. In Rome, everyone is talking about how, last week, he let Senator Titius be seized and executed on the merest suspicion."

"The poor Emperor no longer knows what he does!" exclaimed the young woman; and shook her head in pity and surprise.

"You are perfectly right," said the stranger, as an expression of the deepest melancholy crossed his countenance. "Tiberius knows that everyone hates him, and this is driving him insane."

"What say you?" the woman retorted. "Why should we hate him? We only deplore the fact that he is no longer the great Emperor he was in the beginning of his reign."

"You are mistaken," said the stranger. "Everyone hates and detests Tiberius. Why should they do otherwise? He is nothing but a cruel and merciless tyrant. In Rome they think that from now on he will become even more unreasonable than he has been."

"Has anything happened, then, which will turn him into a worse beast than he is already?" queried the vine-dresser.

When he said this, the wife noticed that the old woman gave him a new warning signal, but so stealthily that he could not see it.

The stranger answered him in a kindly manner, but at the same time a singular smile played about his lips.

"You have heard, perhaps, that until now Tiberius has had a friend in his household on whom he could rely, and who has always told him the truth. All the rest who live in his palace are fortune-hunters and hypocrites, who praise the Emperor's wicked and cunning acts just as much as his good and admirable ones. But there was, as we have said, one alone who never feared to let him know how his conduct was actually regarded. This person, who was more courageous than senators and generals, was the Emperor's old nurse, Faustina."

"I have heard of her," said the labourer. "I've been told that the Emperor has always shown her great friendship."

"Yes, Tiberius knew how to prize her affection and loyalty. He treated this poor peasant woman, who came from a miserable hut in the Sabine mountains, as his second mother. As long as he stayed in Rome, he let her live in a mansion on the Palatine, that he might always have her near him. None of Rome's noble matrons has fared better than she. She was borne through the streets in a litter, and her dress was that of an empress. When the Emperor moved to Capri, she had to accompany him, and he bought a country estate for her there, and filled it with slaves and costly furnishings."

"She has certainly fared well," said the husband.

Now it was he who kept up the conversation with the stranger. The wife sat silent and observed with surprise the change which had come over the old woman. Since the stranger arrived, she had not spoken a word. She had lost her mild and friendly expression. She had pushed her food aside, and sat erect and rigid against the doorpost, and stared straight ahead, with a severe and stony countenance.

"It was the Emperor's intention that she should have a happy life," said the stranger. "But, despite all his kindly acts, she too has deserted him."

The old woman gave a start at these words, but the young one laid her hand quietingly on her arm. Then she began to speak in her soft, sympathetic voice. "I cannot believe that Faustina has been as happy at court as you say," she said, as she turned toward the stranger. "I am sure that she has loved Tiberius as if he had been her own son. I can understand how proud she has been of his noble youth, and I can even understand how it must have grieved her to see him abandon himself in his old age to suspicion and cruelty. She has certainly warned and admonished him every day. It has been for her terrible always to plead in vain. At last she could no longer bear to see him sink lower and lower."

The stranger, astonished, leaned forward a bit when he heard this; but the young woman did not glance up at him. She kept her eyes lowered, and spoke very calmly and gently.

"Perhaps you are right in what you say of the old woman," he replied. "Faustina has really not been happy at court. It seems strange, nevertheless, that she has left the Emperor in his old age when she had endured him the span of a lifetime."

"What say you?" asked the husband. "Has old Faustina left the Emperor?"

"She has stolen away from Capri without anyone's knowledge," said the stranger. "She left just as poor as she came. She has not taken one of her treasures with her."

"And doesn't the Emperor really know where she has gone?" asked the wife.

"No! No one knows for certain what road the old woman has taken. Still, one takes it for granted that she has sought refuge among her native mountains."

"And the Emperor does not know, either, why she has gone away?" asked the young woman.

"No, the Emperor knows nothing of this. He cannot believe she left him because he once told her that she served him for money and gifts only, like all the rest. She knows, however, that he has never doubted her unselfishness. He has hoped all along that she would return to him voluntarily, for no one knows better than she that he is absolutely without friends."

"I do not know her," said the young woman, "But I think I can tell you why she has left the Emperor. The old woman was brought up among these mountains in simplicity and piety, and she has always longed to come back here again. Surely she never would have abandoned the Emperor if he had not insulted her. But I understand that, after this, she feels she has the right to think of herself, since her days are numbered. If I were a poor woman of the mountains, I certainly would have acted as she did. I would have thought that I had done enough when I had served my master during a whole lifetime. I would at last have abandoned luxury and royal favours to give my soul a taste of honour and integrity before it left me for the long journey."

The stranger glanced with a deep and tender sadness at the young woman. "You do not consider that the Emperor's propensities will become worse than ever. Now there is no one who can calm him when suspicion and misanthropy take possession of him. Think of this," he continued, as his melancholy gaze penetrated deeply into the eyes of the young woman, "in all the world there is no one now whom he does not hate; no one whom he does not despise — no one!"

As he uttered these words of bitter despair, the old woman made a sudden movement and turned toward him, but the young woman looked him straight in the eyes and answered: "Tiberius knows that Faustina will come back to him whenever he wishes it. But first she must know that her old eyes need never more behold vice and infamy at his court."

They had all risen during this speech; but the vine-dresser and his wife placed themselves in front of the old woman, as if to shield her.

The stranger did not utter another syllable, but regarded the old woman with a questioning glance. Is this *your* last word also? he seemed to want to say. The old woman's lips quivered, but words would not pass them.

"If the Emperor has loved his old servant, then he can also let her live her last days in peace," said the young woman.

The stranger hesitated still, but suddenly his dark countenance brightened. "My friends," said he, "Whatever one may say of Tiberius there is one thing which he has learned better than others; and that is — renunciation. I have only one thing more to say to you: If this old woman, of whom we have spoken, should come to this hut, receive her well! The Emperor's favour rests upon anyone who succours her."

He wrapped his mantle about him and departed the same way that he had come.

III

After this, the vine-dresser and his wife never again spoke to the old woman about the Emperor. Between themselves they marvelled that she, at her great age, had had the strength to renounce all the wealth and power to which she had become accustomed. "I wonder if she will not soon go back to Tiberius?" they asked themselves. "It is certain that she still loves him. It is in the hope that it will awaken him to reason and enable him to repent of his low conduct, that she has left him."

"A man as old as the Emperor will never begin a new life," said the labourer. "How are you going to rid him of his great contempt for mankind? Who could go to him and teach him to love his fellow man? Until this happens, he cannot be cured of suspicion and cruelty."

"You know that there is one who could actually do it," said the wife. "I often think of how it would turn out, if the two should meet. But God's ways are not our ways."

The old woman did not seem to miss her former life at all. After a time the young wife gave birth to a child. The old woman had the care of it; she seemed so content in consequence that one could have thought she had forgotten all her sorrows.

Once every half-year she used to wrap her long, grey mantle around her, and wander down to Rome. There she did not seek a soul, but went straight to the Forum. Here she stopped outside a little temple, which was erected on one side of the superbly decorated square.

All there was of this temple was an uncommonly large altar, which stood in a marble-paved court, under the open sky. On the top of the altar, Fortuna, the goddess of happiness, was enthroned, and at its foot was a statue of Tiberius. Encircling the court were buildings for the priests, storerooms for fuel, and stalls for the beasts of sacrifice.

Old Faustina's journeys never extended beyond this temple, where those who would pray for the welfare of Tiberius were wont to come. When she cast a glance in there and saw that both the goddess' and the Emperor's statue were wreathed in flowers; that the sacrificial fire burned; that throngs of reverent worshippers were assembled before the altar, and heard the priests' low chants sounding thereabouts, she turned around and went back to the mountains.

In this way she learned, without having to question a human being, that Tiberius was still among the living, and that all was well with him.

The third time she undertook this journey, she met with a surprise. When she reached the little temple, she found it empty and deserted. No fire burned before the statue, and not a worshipper was seen. A couple of dried garlands still hung on one side of the altar, but this was all that testified to its former glory. The priests were gone, and the Emperor's statue, which stood there unguarded, was damaged and mud-bespattered.

The old woman turned to the first passer-by. "What does this mean?" she asked. "Is Tiberius dead? Have we another Emperor?"

"No," replied the Roman, "Tiberius is still Emperor, but we have ceased to pray for him. Our prayers can no longer benefit him."

"My friend," said the old woman, "I live far away among the mountains, where one learns nothing of what happens out in the world. Won't you tell me what dreadful misfortune has overtaken the Emperor?"

"The most dreadful of all misfortunes! He has been stricken with a disease which has never before been known in Italy, but which seems to be common in the Orient. Since this evil has befallen the Emperor, his features are changed, his voice has become like an animal's grunt, and his toes and fingers are rotting away. And for this illness there appears to be no remedy. They believe that he will die within a few weeks. But if he does not die, he will be dethroned, for such an ill and wretched man can no longer conduct the affairs of State. You understand, of course, that his fate is a foregone conclusion. It is useless to invoke the gods for his success, and it is not worthwhile," he added, with a faint smile. "No one has anything more either to fear or hope from him. Why, then, should we trouble ourselves on his account?"

He nodded and walked away; but the old woman stood there as if stunned.

For the first time in her life she collapsed and looked like one whom age has subdued. She stood with bent back and trembling head, and with hands that groped feebly in the air.

She longed to get away from the place, but she moved her feet slowly. She looked around to find something which she could use as a staff.

But after a few moments, by a tremendous effort of the will, she succeeded in conquering the faintness.

IV

A week later, old Faustina wandered up the steep inclines on the Island of Capri. It was a warm day and the dread consciousness of old age and feebleness came over her as she laboured up the winding roads and the hewn-out steps in the mountain, which led to Tiberius's villa.

This feeling increased when she observed how changed everything had become during the time she had been away. In truth, on and alongside these steps there had always before been throngs of people. Here it used fairly to swarm with senators, borne by giant Libyans; with messengers from the provinces attended by long processions of slaves; with office-seekers; with noblemen invited to participate in the Emperor's feasts.

But today the steps and passages were entirely deserted. Grey-greenish lizards were the only living things which the old woman saw in her path.

She was amazed to see that already everything appeared to be going to ruin. At most, the Emperor's illness could not have progressed more than two months, and yet the grass had already taken root in the cracks between the marble stones. Rare growths, planted in beautiful vases, were already withered and here and there mischievous spoilers, whom no one had taken the trouble to stop, had broken down the balustrade.

But to her the most singular thing of all was the entire absence of people. Even if strangers were forbidden to appear on the island, attendants at least should still be found there: the endless crowds of soldiers and slaves; of dancers and musicians; of cooks and stewards; of palace-sentinels and gardeners, who belonged to the Emperor's household.

When Faustina reached the upper terrace, she caught sight of two slaves, who sat on the steps in front of the villa. As she approached, they rose and bowed to her.

"Be greeted, Faustina!" said one of them. "It is a god who sends thee to lighten our sorrows."

"What does this mean, Milo?" asked Faustina. "Why is it so deserted here? Yet they have told me that Tiberius still lives at Capri."

"The Emperor has driven away all his slaves because he suspects that one of us has given him poisoned wine to drink, and that this has brought on the illness. He would have driven even Tito and myself away, if we had not refused to obey him; yet, as you know, we have all our lives served the Emperor and his mother."

"I do not ask after slaves only," said Fuastina. "Where are the senators and field marshals? Where are the Emperor's intimate friends; and all the fawning fortune-hunters?"

"Tiberius does not wish to show himself before strangers," said the slave. "Senator Lucius and Marco, Commander of the Life Guard, come here every day and receive orders. No one else may approach him."

Faustina had gone up the steps to enter the villa. The slave went before her, and on the way she asked: "What say the physicians of Tiberius' illness?"

"None of them understands how to treat this illness. They do not even know if it kills quickly or slowly. But this I can tell you, Faustina, Tiberius must die if he continues to refuse all food for fear it may be poisoned. And I know that a sick man cannot stay awake night and

101

day, as the Emperor does, for fear he may be murdered in his sleep. If he will trust you as in former days, you might succeed in making him eat and sleep. Thereby you can prolong his life for many days."

The slave conducted Faustina through several passages and courts to a terrace which Tiberius used to frequent to enjoy the view of the beautiful bays and proud Vesuvius.

When Faustina stepped out upon the terrace, she saw a hideous creature with a swollen face and animal-like features. His hands and feet were swathed in white bandages, but through the bandages protruded half-rotted fingers and toes. And this being's clothes were soiled and dusty. It was evident he could not walk erect, but had been obliged to crawl out upon the terrace. He lay with closed eyes near the balustrade at the farthest end, and did not move when the slave and Faustina came.

Faustina whispered to the slave, who walked before her: "But, Milo, how can such a creature be found here on the Emperor's private terrace? Make haste, and take him away!"

But she had scarcely said this when she saw the slave bow to the ground before the miserable creature who lay there.

"Caesar Tiberius," said he, "at last I have glad tidings to bring thee."

At the same time the slave turned toward Faustina, but he shrank back, aghast! and could not speak another word.

He did not behold the proud matron who had looked so strong that one might have expected that she would live to the age of a sibyl. In this moment, she had drooped into impotent age, and the slave saw before him a bent old woman with misty eyes and fumbling hands.

Faustina had certainly heard that the Emperor was terribly changed, yet never for a moment had she ceased to think of him as the strong man he was when she last saw him. She had also heard someone say that this illness progressed slowly, and that it took years to transform a human being. But here it had advanced with such virulence that it had made the Emperor unrecognizable in just two months.

She tottered up to the Emperor. She could not speak, but stood silent beside him, and wept.

"Are you come now, Faustina?" he said, without opening his eyes. "I lay and fancied that you stood here and wept over me. I dare not look up for fear I will find that it was only an illusion.

Then the old woman sat down beside him. She raised his head and placed it on her knee.

But Tiberius lay still, without looking at her. A sense of sweet repose enfolded him, and the next moment he sank into a peaceful slumber.

V

A few weeks later, one of the Emperor's slaves came to the lonely hut in the Sabine mountains. It drew on toward evening, and the vine-dresser and his wife stood in the doorway and saw the sun set in the distant west. The slave turned out of the path, and came up and greeted them. Thereupon he took a heavy purse, which he carried in his girdle, and laid it in the husband's hand.

"This, Faustina, the old woman to whom you have shown compassion, sends you," said the slave. "She begs that with this money you will purchase a vineyard of your own, and build a house that does not lie as high in the air as the eagles' nests."

"Old Faustina still lives, then?" said the husband. "We have searched for her in cleft and morass. When she did not come back to us, I thought that she had met her death in these wretched mountains.

"Don't you remember," the wife interposed, "that I would not believe that she was dead? Did I not say to you that she had gone back to the Emperor?"

This the husband admitted. "And I am glad," he added, "that you were right, not only because Faustina has become rich enough to help us out of our poverty, but also on the poor Emperor's account."

The slave wanted to say farewell at once, in order to reach densely-settled quarters before dark, but this the couple would not permit. "You must stop with us until morning," said they. "We cannot let you go before you have told us all that has happened to Faustina. Why has she returned to the Emperor? What was their meeting like? Are they glad to be together again?"

The slave yielded to these solicitations. He followed them into the hut, and during the evening meal he told them all about the Emperor's illness and Faustina's return.

When the slave had finished his narrative, he saw that both the man and the woman sat motionless — dumb with amazement. Their gaze was fixed on the ground, as though not to betray the emotion which affected them.

Finally the man looked up and said to his wife: "Don't you believe God has decreed this?" — "Yes," said the wife, "surely it was for this that our Lord sent us across the sea to this lonely hut. Surely this was His purpose when He sent the old woman to our door."

As soon as the wife had spoken these words, the vine-dresser turned again to the slave.

"Friend!" he said to him, "you shall carry a message from me to Faustina. Tell her this word for word! Thus your friend the vineyard labourer from the Sabine mountains greets you. You have seen the young woman, my wife. Did she not appear fair to you, and blooming with health? And yet this young woman once suffered from the same disease which now has stricken Tiberius."

104

The slave made a gesture of surprise, but the vine-dresser continued with greater emphasis on his words.

"If Faustina refuses to believe my word, tell her that my wife and I came from Palestine, in Asia, a land where this disease is common. There the law is such that the lepers are driven from the cities and towns, and must live in tombs and mountain grottoes. Tell Faustina that my wife was born of diseased parents in a mountain grotto. As long as she was a child she was healthy, but when she grew up into young maidenhood she was stricken with the disease."

The slave bowed, smiled pleasantly, and said: "How can you expect that Faustina will believe this? She has seen your wife in her beauty and health. And she must know that there is no remedy for this illness."

The man replied: "It were best for her that she believed me. But I am not without witnesses. She can send inquiries over to Nazareth, in Galilee. There every one will confirm my statement."

"Is it perchance through a miracle of some god that your wife has been cured?" asked the slave.

"Yes, it is as you say," answered the labourer. "One day a rumour reached the sick who lived in the wilderness: 'Behold, a great Prophet has arisen in Nazareth of Galilee. He is filled with the power of God's Spirit, and he can cure your illness just by laying his hand upon your forehead!' But the sick who lay in their misery would not believe that this rumour was the truth. 'No one can heal us,' they said. 'Since the days of the great prophets no one has been able to save one of us from this misfortune.'

"But there was one amongst them who believed, and that was a young maiden. She left the others to seek her way to the city of Nazareth, where the Prophet lived. One day, when she wandered over wide plains, she met a man tall of stature, with a pale face and hair which lay in even, black curls. His dark eyes shone like stars and drew her toward him. But before they met, she called out to him: 'Come not near me, for I am unclean, but tell me where I can find the Prophet from Nazareth!' But the man continued to walk towards her, and when he stood directly in front of her, he said: 'Why seekest thou the Prophet of Nazareth?' — 'I seek him that he may lay his hand on my forehead and heal me of my illness.' Then the man went up and laid his hand upon her brow. But she said to him: 'What doth it avail me that you lay your hand upon my forehead? You surely are no prophet?' Then he smiled on her and said: 'Go now into the city which lies yonder at the foot of the mountain, and show thyself before the priests!'

''The sick maiden thought to herself: 'He mocks me because I believe I can be healed. From him I cannot learn what I would know.' And she went farther. Soon thereafter she saw a man, who was going out to hunt, riding across the wide field. When he came so near that he could hear her, she called to him: 'Come not close to me, I am unclean! But tell me where I can find the Prophet of Nazareth!' — 'What do you want of the Prophet?' asked the man, riding slowly toward her. 'I wish only that he might lay his hand on my forehead and heal me of my illness.' The man rode still nearer. 'Of what illness do you wish to be healed?' said he. 'Surely you need no physician!' — 'Can't you see than I am a leper?' said she. 'I was born of diseased parents in a mountain grotto.' But the man continued to approach, for she was beautiful and fair, like a new-blown rose. 'You are the most beautiful maiden in Judaea!' he exclaimed. 'Ah, taunt me not — you, too!' said she. 'I know that my features are destroyed, and that my voice is like a wild beast's growl.'

''He looked deep into her eyes and said to her: 'Your voice is as resonant as the spring brook's when it ripples over pebbles, and your face is as smooth as a coverlet of soft satin.'

''That moment he rode so close to her than she could see her face

in the shining mountings which decorated his saddle. 'You shall look at yourself here,' said he. She did so, and saw a face smooth and soft as a newly-formed butterfly wing. 'What is this that I see?' she said. 'This is not my face!' — 'Yes, it is your face,' said the rider. 'But my voice, is it not rough? Does it not sound as when wagons are drawn over a stony road?' — 'No! It sounds like a zither player's sweetest songs,' said the rider.

"She turned and pointed toward the road. 'Do you know who that man is just disappearing behind the two oaks?' she asked.

" 'It is he whom you lately asked after; it is the Prophet from Nazareth,' said the man. Then she clasped her hands in astonishment and tears filled her eyes. 'Oh, thou Holy One! Oh, thou Messenger of God's power!' she cried. 'Thou hast healed me!'

"Then the rider lifted her into the saddle and bore her to the city at the foot of the mountain and went with her to the priests and elders, and told them how he had found her. They questioned her carefully; but when they heard that the maiden was born in the wilderness of diseased parents, they would not believe that she was healed. 'Go back thither whence you came!' said they. 'If you have been ill, you must remain so as long as you live. You must not come here to the city, to infect the rest of us with your disease.'

"She said to them, 'I know that I am well, for the Prophet from Nazareth hath laid his hand upon my forehead.'

"When they heard this they exclaimed: 'Who is he, that he should be able to make clean the unclean? All this is but a delusion of the evil spirits. Go back to your own, that you may not bring destruction upon all of us!'

"They would not declare her healed, and they forbade her to remain in the city. They decreed that each and everyone who gave her shelter should also be adjudged unclean.

"When the priests had pronounced this judgment, the young

maiden turned to the man who had found her in the field: 'Whither shall I go now? Must I go back again to the lepers in the wilderness?'

"But the man lifted her once more upon his horse, and said to her: 'No, under no conditions shall you go out to the lepers in their mountain caves, but we two shall travel across the sea to another land, where there are no laws for clean and unclean.' And they —"

But when the vineyard labourer had got thus far in his narrative, the slave arose and interrupted him. "You need not tell any more," said he. "Stand up rather and follow me on the way, you who know the mountains, so that I can begin my home journey tonight, and not wait until morning. The Emperor and Faustina cannot hear your tidings a moment too soon."

When the vine-dresser had accompanied the slave, and come home again to the hut, he found his wife still awake.

"I cannot sleep," said she. "I am thinking that these two will meet: he who loves all mankind, and he who hates them. Such a meeting would be enough to sweep the earth out of existence!"

VI

Old Faustina was in distant Palestine, on her way to Jerusalem. She had not desired that the mission to seek the Prophet and bring him to the Emperor should be entrusted to anyone but herself. She said to herself: "That which we demand of this stranger, is something which we cannot coax from him either by force or bribes. But perhaps he will grant it us if someone falls at his feet and tells him in what dire need the Emperor is. Who can make an honest plea for Tiberius, but the one who suffers from his misfortune as much as he does?"

The hope of possibly saving Tiberius had renewed the old

woman's youth. She withstood without difficulty the long sea trip to Joppa and on the journey to Jerusalem she made no use of a litter, but rode a horse. She appeared to stand the difficult ride as easily as the Roman nobles, the soldiers, and the slaves who made up retinue.

The journey from Joppa to Jerusalem filled the old woman's heart with joy and bright hopes. It was springtime, and Sharon's plain, over which they had ridden during the first day's travel, had been a brilliant carpet of flowers. Even during the second day's journey, when they came to the hills of Judaea, they were not abandoned by the flowers. All the multiformed hills between which the road wound were planted with fruit trees, which stood in full bloom. And when the travellers wearied of looking at the white and red blossoms of the apricots and persimmons, they could rest their eyes by observing the young vine-leaves, which pushed their way through the dark brown branches, and their growth was so rapid that one could almost follow it with the eye.

It was not only flowers and spring green that made the journey pleasant, but the pleasure was enhanced by watching the throngs of people who were on their way to Jerusalem this morning. From all the roads and by-paths, from lonely heights, and from the most remote corners of the plain came travellers. When they had reached the road to Jerusalem, those who travelled alone formed themselves into companies and marched forward with glad shouts. Round an elderly man, who rode on a jogging camel, walked his sons and daughters, his sons-in-law and daughters-in-law, and all his grandchildren. It was such a large family that it made up an entire little village. An old grandmother who was too feeble to walk her sons had taken in their arms, and with pride she let herself be borne among the crowds, who respectfully stepped aside.

In truth, it was a morning to inspire joy even in the most disconsolate. To be sure the sky was not clear, but was overcast with a thin greyish-white mist, but none of the wayfarers thought of grumbling because the sun's piercing brilliancy was dampened. Under this veiled sky the perfume of the budding leaves and blossoms did not penetrate the air as usual, but lingered over roads and fields. And this beautiful day, with its faint mist and hushed winds, which reminded one of Night's rest and calm, seemed to communicate to the hastening crowds somewhat of itself, so that they went forward happy — yet with solemnity — singing in subdued voices ancient hymns, or playing upon peculiar old-fashioned instruments, from which came tones like the buzzing of gnats, or grasshoppers' piping.

When old Faustina rode forward among all the people, she became infected with their joy and excitement. She prodded her horse to quicker speed, as she said to a young Roman who rode beside her: "I dreamt last night that I saw Tiberius, and he implored me not to postpone the journey, but to ride to Jerusalem today. It appears as if the gods had wished to send me a warning not to neglect to go there this beautiful morning."

Just as she said this, she came to the top of a long mountain ridge, and there she was obliged to halt. Before her lay a large, deep valley-basin, surrounded by pretty hills, and from the dark, shadowy depths of the vale rose the massive mountain which held on its head the city of Jerusalem.

But the narrow mountain city, with its walls and towers, which lay like a jewelled coronet upon the cliff's smooth height, was this day magnified a thousand-fold. All the hills which encircled the valley were bedecked with gay tents, and with a swarm of human beings.

It was evident to Faustina that all the inhabitants were on their way to Jerusalem to celebrate some great holiday. Those from a distance had already come, and had managed to put their tents in order. On the other hand those who lived near the city were still on their way. Along all the shining rock-heights one saw them come streaming in

111

like an unbroken sea of white robes, of songs, of holiday cheer.

For some time the old woman surveyed these seething throngs of people and the long rows of tent-poles. Thereupon she said to the young Roman who rode beside her:

"Verily, Sulpicius, the whole nation must have come to Jerusalem."

"It really appears like it," replied the Roman, who had been chosen by Tiberius to accompany Faustina because he had, during a number of years, lived in Judaea. "They celebrate now the great Spring Festival, and at this time all the people, both old and young, come to Jerusalem."

Faustina reflected a moment. "I am glad that we came to this city on the day that the people celebrate their festival," said she. "It cannot signify anything else than that the gods protect our journey. Do you think it likely that he whom we seek, the Prophet of Nazareth, has also come to Jerusalem to participate in the festivities?"

"You are surely right, Faustina," said the Roman. "He must be here in Jerusalem. This is indeed a decree of the gods. Strong and vigorous though you be, you may consider yourself fortunate if you escape making the long and troublesome journey up to Galilee."

At once he rode over to a couple of wayfarers and asked them if they thought the Prophet of Nazareth was in Jerusalem.

"We have seen him here every day at this season," answered one. "Surely he must be here even this year, for he is a holy and righteous man."

A woman stretched forth her hand and pointed towards a hill, which lay east of the city. "Do you see the foot of that mountain, which is covered with olive trees?" she said. "It is there that the Galileans usually raise their tents, and there you will get the most reliable information about him whom you seek."

They journeyed farther, and travelled on a winding path all the way down to the bottom of the valley, and then they began to ride up toward Zion's hill, to reach the city on its heights. The woman who had spoken went along the same way.

The steep ascending road was encompassed here by low walls, and upon these countless beggars and cripples sat or lolled. "Look," said the woman who had spoken, pointing to one of the beggars who sat on the wall, "There is a Galilean! I recollect that I have seen him among the Prophet's disciples. He can tell you where you will find him you seek."

Faustina and Sulpicius rode up to the man who had been pointed out to her. He was a poor old man with a heavy iron-grey beard. His face was bronzed by heat and sunshine. He asked no alms; on the contrary, he was so engrossed in anxious thought that he did not even glance at the passers-by.

Nor did he hear that Sulpicius addressed him and the latter had to repeat his question several times.

"My friend, I've been told that you are a Galilean. I beg you, therefore, to tell me where I shall find the Prophet from Nazareth!"

The Galilean gave a sudden start and looked around him, confused. But when he finally comprehended what was wanted of him, he was seized with rage mixed with terror. "What are you talking about?" he burst out. "Why do you ask me about that man? I know nothing of him. I'm not a Galilean."

The Hebrew woman now joined in the conversation. "Still I have seen you in his company," she protested. "Do not fear, but tell this noble Roman lady, who is the Emperor's friend, where she is most likely to find him."

But the terrified disciple grew more and more irascible. "Have all the people gone mad today?" said he. "Are they possessed by an evil spirit, since they come again and again and ask me about that man?

Why will no one believe me when I say that I do not know the Prophet? I do not come from his country. I have never seen him."

His irritability attracted attention, and a couple of beggars who sat on the wall beside him also began to dispute his word.

"Certainly you were among his disciples," said one. "We all know that you came with him from Galilee."

Then the man raised his arms toward heaven and cried: "I could not endure it in Jerusalem today on that man's account, and now they will not even leave me in peace out here among the beggars! Why don't you believe me when I say to you that I have never seen him?"

Faustina turned away with a shrug. "Let us go farther!" said she. "The man is mad. From him we will learn nothing."

They went farther up the mountain. Faustina was not more than two steps from the city gate, when the Hebrew woman who had wished to help her find the Prophet called to her to be careful. She pulled in her reins and saw that a man lay in the road, just in front of the horse's feet, where the crush was greatest. It was a miracle that he had not already been trampled to death by animals or people.

The man lay upon his back and stared upward with lustreless eyes. He did not move, although the camels placed their heavy feet close beside him. He was poorly clad, and besides he was covered with dust and dirt. In fact, he had thrown so much gravel over himself that it looked as if he tried to hide himself, to be more easily over-ridden and trampled down.

"What does this mean? Why does this man lie here on the road?" asked Faustina.

Instantly the man began shouting to the passers-by:

"In mercy, brothers and sisters, drive your horses and camels over me! Do not turn aside for me! Trample me to dust! I have betrayed innocent blood. Trample me to dust!"

Sulpicius caught Faustina's horse by the bridle and turned it to one side. "It is a sinner who wants to do penance," said he. "Do not let this delay your journey. These people are peculiar and one must let them follow their own bent."

The man in the road continued to shout: "Set your heels on my heart! Let the camels cruch my breast and the asses dig their hoofs into my eyes!"

But Faustina seemed loath to ride past the miserable man without trying to make him rise. She remained all the while beside him.

The Hebrew woman who had wished to serve her once before, pushed her way forward again. "This man also belonged to the Prophet's disciples," said she. "Do you wish me to ask him about his Master?"

Faustina nodded affirmatively, and the woman bent down over the man.

"What have you Galileans done this day with your Master?" she asked. "I meet you scattered on highways and byways, but him I see nowhere."

But when she questioned in this manner, the man who lay in the dust rose to his knees. "What evil spirit hath possessed you to ask me about him?" he said, in a voice that was filled with despair. "You see, surely, that I have lain down in the road to be trampled to death. Is not that enough for you? Shall you come also and ask me what I have done with him?"

When she repeated the question, the man staggered to his feet and put both hands to his ears.

"Woe unto you, that you cannot let me die in peace!" he cried. He forced his way through the crowds that thronged in front of the gate, and rushed away shrieking with terror, while his torn robe fluttered around him like dark wings.

"It appears to me as though we had come to a nation of madmen," said Faustina, when she saw the man flee. She had become depressed by seeing these disciples of the Prophet. Could the man who numbered such fools among his followers do anything for the Emperor?

Even the Hebrew woman looked distressed, and she said very earnestly to Faustina: "Mistress, delay not in your search for him whom you would find! I fear some evil has befallen him, since his disciples are beside themselves and cannot bear to hear him spoken of."

Faustina and her retinue finally rode through the gate archway and came in on the narrow and dark streets, which were alive with people. It seemed well-nigh impossible to get through the city. The riders time and again had to stand still. Slaves and soldiers tried in vain to clear the way. The people continued to rush on in a compact irresistible stream.

"Verily," said the old woman, "the streets of Rome are peaceful gardens compared with these!"

Sulpicius soon saw that almost insurmountable difficulties awaited them.

"On these overcrowded streets it is easier to walk than to ride," said he. "If you are not too fatigued, I should advise you to walk to the Governor's palace. It is a good distance away, but if we ride we certainly will not get there until after midnight."

Faustina accepted the suggestion at once. She dismounted, and left her horse with one of the slaves. Thereupon the Roman travellers began to walk through the city.

This was much better. They pushed their way quickly toward the heart of the city, and Sulpicius showed Faustina a rather wide street which they were nearing.

"Look, Faustina," he said, "if we take this street, we will soon be there. It leads directly down to our quarters."

116

But just as they were about to turn into the street, the worst obstacle met them.

It happened that the very moment when Faustina reached the street which extended from the Governor's palace to Righteousness' Gate and Golgotha, they brought through it a prisoner, who was to be taken out and crucified. Before him ran a crowd of wild youths who wanted to witness the execution. They raced up the street, waved their arms in rapture towards the hill, and emitted unintelligible howls — in their delight at being allowed to view something which they did not see every day.

Behind them came companies of men in silken robes, who appeared to belong to the city's elite and foremost. Then came women, many of whom had tear-stained faces. A gathering of poor and maimed staggered forward, uttering shrieks that pierced the ears.

"O God!" they cried, "save him! Send Thine angel and save him! Send a deliverer in his direst need!"

Finally, there came a few Roman soldiers on great horses. They kept guard so that none of the people could dash up to the prisoner and try to rescue him.

Directly behind them followed the executioners, whose task it was to lead forward the man that was to be crucified. They had laid a heavy wooden cross over his shoulder, but he was too weak for this burden. It weighed him down so that his body was almost bent to the ground. He held his head down so far that no one could see his face.

Faustina stood at the opening of the little by-street and saw the doomed man's heavy tread. She noticed, with surprise, that he wore a purple mantle, and that a crown of thorns was pressed down upon his head.

"Who is this man?" she asked. One of the bystanders answered her: "It is one who wished to make himself Emperor."

"And must he suffer death for a thing which is scarcely worth striving after?" said the old woman sadly.

The doomed man staggered under the cross. He dragged himself forward more and more slowly. The executioners had tied a rope around his waist, and they began to pull on it to hasten the speed. But as they pulled the rope the man fell, and lay there with the cross over him.

There was a terrible uproar. The Roman soldiers had all they could do to hold the crowds back. They drew their swords on a couple of women who tried to rush forward to help the fallen man. The executioners attempted to force him up with cuffs and lashes, but he could not move because of the cross. Finally two of them took hold of the cross to remove it.

Then he raised his head, and old Faustina could see his face. The cheeks were streaked by lashes from a whip, and from his brow, which was wounded by the thorn-crown, trickled some drops of blood. His hair hung in knotted tangles, clotted with sweat and blood. His jaw was firm set, but his lips trembled, as if they struggled to suppress a cry. His eyes, tear-filled and almost blinded from torture and fatigue, stared straight ahead.

But behind this half-dead person's face, the old woman saw — as in a vision — a pale and beautiful One with glorious, majestic eyes and gentle features, and she was seized with sudden grief — touched by the unknown man's misfortune and degradation.

"Oh, what have they done with you, you poor soul!" she burst out, and moved a step nearer him, while her eyes filled with tears. She forgot her own sorrow and anxiety for this tortured man's distress. She thought her heart would burst from pity. She, like the other women, wanted to rush forward and tear him away from the executioners!

The fallen man saw how she came toward him, and he crept

118

closer to her. It was as though he had expected to find protection with her against all those who persecuted and tortured him. He embraced her knees. He pressed himself against her, like a child who clings close to his mother for safety.

The old woman bent over him, and as the tears streamed down her cheeks, she felt the most blissful joy because he had come and sought protection with her. She placed one arm around his neck, and as a mother first of all wipes away the tears from her child's eyes, she laid her kerchief of sheer fine linen over his face, to wipe away the tears and the blood.

But now the executioners were ready with the cross. They came now and snatched away the prisoner. Impatient over the delay, they dragged him off in wild haste. The condemned man uttered a groan when he was led away from the refuge he had found, but he made no resistance.

Faustina embraced him to hold him back, and when her feeble old hands were powerless and she saw him borne away, she felt as if some one had torn from her her own child, and she cried: "No, no! Do not take him from me! He must not die! He shall not die!"

She felt the most intense grief and indignation because he was being led away. She wanted to rush after him. She wanted to fight with the executioners and tear him from them.

But with the first step she took, she was seized with weakness and dizziness. Sulpicius made haste to place his arm around her, to prevent her from falling.

On one side of the street he saw a little shop, and carried her in. There was neither bench nor chair inside, but the shopkeeper was a kindly man. He helped her over to a rug, and arranged a bed for her on the stone floor.

She was not unconscious, but such a great dizziness had seized her that she could not sit up, but was forced to lie down.

"She has made a long journey today, and the noise and crush in the city have been too much for her," said Sulpicius to the merchant. "She is very old, and no one is so strong as not to be conquered by age."

"This is a trying day, even for one who is not old," said the merchant. "The air is almost too heavy to breathe. It would not surprise me if a severe storm were in store for us."

Sulpicius bent over the old woman. She had fallen asleep, and she slept with calm, regular respirations after all the excitement and fatigue.

He walked over to the shop door, stood there, and looked at the crowds while he awaited her waking.

VII

The Roman governor at Jerusalem had a young wife, and she had had a dream during the night preceding the day when Faustina entered the city.

She dreamed that she stood on the roof of her house and looked down upon the beautiful court, which according to the Oriental custom, was paved with marble, and planted with rare growths.

But in the court she saw assembled all the sick and blind and halt there were in the world. She saw before her the pest-ridden with bodies swollen with boils, lepers with disfigured faces, the paralytics, who could not move, but lay helpless upon the ground, and all the wretched creatures who writhed in torment and pain.

They all crowded up towards the entrance, to get into the house; and a number of those who walked foremost pounded on the palace door.

At last she saw that a slave opened the door and came out on the threshold, and she heard him ask what they wanted.

Then they answered him, saying: "We seek the great Prophet

121

whom God hath sent to the world. Where is the Prophet of Nazareth, he who is master of all suffering? Where is he who can deliver us from all our torment?'''

Then the slave answered them in an arrogant and indifferent tone — as palace servants do when they turn away the poor stranger:

"It will profit you nothing to seek the great Prophet. Pilate has killed him."

Then there arose among all the sick a grief and a moaning and a gnashing of teeth which she could not bear to hear. Her heart was wrung with compassion, and tears streamed from her eyes. But when she had begun to weep, she awakened.

Again she fell asleep; and again she dreamed that she stood on the roof of her house and looked down upon the big court, which was as broad as a square.

And behold! the court was filled with all the insane and soul-sick and those possessed of evil spirits. And she saw those who were naked and those who were covered with their long hair and those who had braided themselves crowns of straw and mantles of grass and believed they were kings, and those who crawled on the ground and thought themselves beasts, and those who came dragging heavy stones, which they believed to be gold, and those who thought that the evil spirits spoke through their mouths.

She saw all these crowd up toward the palace gate. And the ones who stood nearest to it knocked and pounded to get in.

At last the door opened, and a slave stepped out on the threshold and asked: "What do you want?"

Then all began to cry aloud, saying: "Where is the great Prophet of Nazareth, he who was sent of God, and who shall restore to us our souls and our wits?"

She heard the slave answer them in the most indifferent tone: "It is useless for you to seek the great Prophet, Pilate has killed him.''

When this was said, they uttered a shriek as wild as a beast's howl, and in their despair they began to lacerate themselves until the blood ran down on the stones. And when she who dreamed saw their distress, she wrung her hands and moaned. And her own moans awakened her.

But again she fell asleep, and again, in her dream, she was on the roof of her house. Round about her sat her slaves, who played for her upon cymbals and zithers, and the almond trees shook their white blossoms over her, and clambering rose-vines exhaled their perfume.

As she sat there, a voice spoke to her: ''Go over to the balustrade which encloses the roof, and see who they are that stand and wait in your court!'' But in the dream she declined, and said: ''I do not care to see any more of those who throng my court tonight.''

Just then she heard a clanking of chains and a pounding of heavy hammers, and the pounding of wood against wood. Her slaves ceased their singing and playing and hurried over to the railing and looked down. Nor could she herself remain seated, but walked thither and looked down on the court.

Then she saw that the court was filled with all the poor prisoners in the world. She saw those who must lie in dark prison dungeons, fettered with heavy chains; she saw those who laboured in the dark mines come dragging their heavy planks, and those who were rowers on war galleys come with their heavy iron-bound oars. And those who were condemned to be crucified came dragging their crosses, and those who were to be beheaded came with their broad-axes. She saw those who were sent into slavery to foreign lands and whose eyes burned with homesickness. She saw those who must serve as beasts of burden, and whose backs were bleeding from lashes.

123

All these unfortunates cried as with one voice: "Open, open!"

Then the slave who guarded the entrance stepped to the door and asked: "What is it that you wish?"

And these answered like the others: "We seek the great Prophet of Nazareth, who has come to the world to give the prisoners their freedom and the slaves their lost happiness."

The slave answered them in a tired and indifferent tone: "You cannot find him here. Pilate has killed him."

When this was said, she who dreamed thought that among all the unhappy there arose such an outburst of scorn and blasphemy that heaven and earth trembled. She was ice-cold with fright, and her body shook so that she awakened.

When she was thoroughly awake, she sat up in bed and thought to herself: "I would not dream more. Now I want to remain awake all night, that I may escape seeing more of this horror."

And even whilst she was thinking thus, drowsiness crept in upon her anew, and she laid her head on the pillow and fell asleep.

Again she dreamed that she sat on the roof of her house, and now her little son ran back and forth up there, and played with a ball.

Then she heard a voice that said to her: "Go over to the balustrade, which encloses the roof, and see who they are that stand and wait in your court!" But she who dreamed said to herself: "I have seen enough misery this night. I cannot endure any more. I would remain where I am."

At that moment her son threw his ball so that it dropped outside the balustrade, and the child ran forward and clambered up on the railing. Then she was frightened. She rushed over and seized hold of the child.

But with that she happened to cast her eyes downward, and once more she saw that the court was full of people.

In the court were all the peoples of earth who had been wounded in battle. They came with severed bodies, with cut-off limbs, and with big open wounds from which the blood oozed, so that the whole court was drenched with it.

And beside these, came all the people in the world who had lost their loved ones on the battlefield. They were the fatherless who mourned their protectors, and the young maidens who cried for their lovers, and the aged who sighed for their sons.

The foremost among them pushed against the door, and the watchman came out as before, and opened it.

He asked all these, who had been wounded in battles and skirmishes: "What seek ye in this house?"

And they answered: "We seek the great Prophet of Nazareth, who shall prohibit wars and rumours of wars and bring peace to the earth. We seek him who shall convert spears into scythes and swords into pruning hooks."

Then answered the slave somewhat impatiently: "Let no more come to pester me! I have already said it often enough. The great Prophet is not here. Pilate has killed him."

Thereupon he closed the gate. But she who dreamed thought of all the lamentation which would come now. "I do not wish to hear it," said she, and rushed away from the balustrade. That instant she awoke. Then she discovered that in her terror she had jumped out of her bed and down on the cold stone floor.

Again she thought she did not want to sleep more that night, and again sleep overpowered her, and she closed her eyes and began to dream.

She sat once more on the roof of her house, and beside her stood her husband. She told him of her dreams, and he ridiculed her.

Again she heard a voice, which said to her: "Go see the people who wait in your court!" But she thought: "I would not see them. I have seen enough misery tonight."

Just then she heard three loud raps on the gate, and her husband walked over to the balustrade to see who it was that asked admittance to his house.

But no sooner had he leaned over the railing, than he beckoned to his wife to come over to him.

"Know you not this man?" said he, and pointed down.

When she looked down on the court, she found that it was filled with horses and riders, slaves were busy unloading asses and camels. It looked as though a distinguished traveller might have landed.

At the entrance gate stood the traveller. He was a large elderly man with broad shoulders and a heavy and gloomy appearance.

The dreamer recognized the stranger instantly, and whispered to her husband: "It is Caesar Tiberius, who is here in Jerusalem. It cannot be anyone else."

"I also seem to recognize him," said her husband; at the same time he placed his finger on his mouth, as a signal that they should be quiet and listen to what was said down in the court.

They saw that the doorkeeper came out and asked the stranger: "Whom seek you?"

And the traveller answered: "I seek the great Prophet of Nazareth, who is endowed with God's power to perform miracles. It is Emperor Tiberius who calls him, that he may liberate him from a terrible disease, which no other physician can cure."

When he had spoken, the slave bowed very humbly and said: "My lord, be not wroth! but your wish cannot be fulfilled."

Then the Emperor turned toward his slaves, who waited below in the court, and gave them a command.

Then the slaves hastened forward—some with handfuls of ornaments, others carried goblets studded with pearls, others again dragged sacks filled with gold coin.

126

The Emperor turned to the slave who guarded the gate, and said: "All this shall be his, if he helps Tiberius. With this he can give riches to all the world's poor."

But the doorkeeper bowed still lower and said: "Master, be not wroth with thy servant, but thy request cannot be fulfilled."

Then the Emperor beckoned again to his slaves, and a pair of them hurried forward with a richly embroidered robe, upon which glittered a breast-piece of jewels.

And the Emperor said to the slave: "See! This which I offer him is the power over Judaea. He shall rule his people like the highest judge, if he will only come and heal Tiberius!"

The slave bowed still nearer the earth, and said: "Master, it is not within my power to help you."

Then the Emperor beckoned once again, and his slaves rushed up with a golden coronet and a purple mantle.

"See," he said, "this is the Emperor's will: He promises to appoint the Prophet his successor, and give him dominion over the world. He shall have power to rule the world according to his God's will, if he will only stretch forth his hand and heal Tiberius!"

Then the slave fell at the Emperor's feet and said in an imploring tone: "Master, it does not lie in my power to attend to thy command. He whom thou seekest is no longer here. Pilate has killed him."

VIII

When the young woman awoke, it was already full, clear day, and her female slaves stood and waited that they might help her dress.

She was very silent while she dressed, but finally she asked the slave who arranged her hair, if her husband was up. She learned that he had been called out to pass judgment on a criminal. "I should have liked to talk with him," said the young woman.

"Mistress," said the slave, "it will be difficult to do so during the trial. We will let you know as soon as it is over."

She sat silent now until her toilet was completed. Then she asked: "Has any among you heard of the Prophet of Nazareth?"

"The Prophet of Nazareth is a Jewish miracle-performer," answered one of the slaves instantly.

"It is strange, Mistress, that you should ask after him today," said another slave. "It is just he whom the Jews have brought here to the palace, to let him be tried by the Governor.'

She bade them go at once and ascertain for what cause he was arraigned, and one of the slaves withdrew. When she returned she said: "They accuse him of wanting to make himself king over this land, and they entreat the Governor to let him be crucified."

When the Governor's wife heard this, she grew terrified and said: "I must speak with my husband, otherwise a terrible calamity will happen here this day."

When the slaves said once again that this was impossible, she began to weep and shudder. And one among them was touched, so she said: "If you will send a written message to the Governor, I will try and take it to him."

Immediately she took a stylus and wrote a few words on a wax tablet, and this was given to Pilate.

But him she did not meet alone the whole day; for when he had dismissed the Jews, and the condemned man was taken to the place of execution, the hour for repast was come, and to this Pilate had invited a few of the Romans who visited Jerusalem at this season. They were the commander of the troops and a young instructor in oratory, and several others besides.

This repast was not very gay, for the Governor's wife sat all the while silent and dejected, and took no part in the conversation.

When the guests asked if she was ill or distraught, the Governor

128

laughingly related about the message she had sent him in the morning. He chaffed her because she had believed that a Roman governor would let himself be guided in his judgments by a woman's dreams.

She answered gently and sadly: "In truth, it was no dream, but a warning sent by the gods. You should at least have let the man live through this one day."

They saw that she was seriously distressed. She would not be comforted, no matter how much the guests exerted themselves, by keeping up the conversation to make her forget these empty fancies.

But after a while one of them raised his head and exclaimed: "What is this? Have we sat so long at table that the day is already gone?"

All looked up now, and they observed that a dim twilight settled down over nature. Above all, it was remarkable to see how the whole variegated play of colour which it spread over all creatures and objects, faded away slowly, so that all looked a uniform grey.

Like everything else, even their own faces lost their colour. "We actually look like the dead," said the young orator with a shudder. "Our cheeks are grey and our lips black."

As this darkness grew more intense, the woman's fear increased. "Oh, my friend!" she burst out at last. "Can't you perceive even now that the Immortals would warn you? They are incensed because you condemned a holy and innocent man. I am thinking that although he may already be on the cross, he is surely not dead yet. Let him be taken down from the cross! I would with mine own hands nurse his wounds. Only grant that he be called back to life!"

But Pilate answered laughingly: "You are surely right in that this is a sign from the gods. But they do not let the sun lose its lustre because a Jewish heretic has been condemned to the cross. On the contrary, we may expect that important matters shall appear, which concern the whole kingdom. Who can tell how long old Tiberius — "

He did not finish the sentence, for the darkness had become so profound he could not see even the wine goblet standing in front of him. He broke off, therefore, to order the slaves to fetch some lamps instantly.

When it had become so light that he could see the faces of his guests, it was impossible for him not to notice the depression which had come over them. "Mark you!" he said half-angrily to his wife. "Now it is apparent to me that you have succeeded with your dreams in driving away the joys of the table. But if it must needs be that you cannot think of anything else today, then let us hear what you have dreamed. Tell it us and we will try to interpret its meaning!"

For this the young wife was ready at once. And while she related vision after vision, the guests grew more and more serious. They ceased emptying their goblets, and they sat with brows knit. The only one who continued to laugh and to call the whole thing madness, was the Governor himself.

When the narrative was ended, the young rhetorician said: "Truly, this is something more than a dream, for I have seen this day not the Emperor, but his old friend Faustina, march into the city. Only it surprises me that she has not already appeared in the Governor's palace."

"There is actually a rumour abroad to the effect that the Emperor has been stricken with a terrible illness," observed the leader of the troops. "It also seems very possible to me that your wife's dream may be a god-sent warning."

"There's nothing incredible in this, that Tiberius has sent messengers after the Prophet to summon him to his sick-bed," agreed the young rhetorician.

The Commander turned with profound seriousness toward Pilate. "If the Emperor has actually taken it into his head to let this miracle-worker be summoned, it were better for you and for all of us that he found him alive."

Pilate answered irritably: "Is it the darkness that has turned you into children? One would think that you had all been transformed into dream-interpreters and prophets."

But the courtier continued his argument: "It may not be impossible, perhaps, to save the man's life, if you sent a swift messenger."

"You want to make a laughing-stock of me," answered the Governor. "Tell me, what would become of law and order in this land, if they learned that the Governor pardoned a criminal because his wife has dreamed a bad dream?"

"It is the truth, however, and not a dream, that I have seen Faustina in Jerusalem," said the young orator.

"I shall take the responsibility of defending my actions before the Emperor," said Pilate. "He will understand that this visionary who let himself be misused by my soldiers without resistance, would not have had the power to help him."

As he was speaking, the house was shaken by a noise like a powerful rolling thunder, and an earthquake shook the ground. The Governor's palace stood intact, but during some minutes just after the earthquake, a terrific crash of crumbling houses and falling pillars was heard.

As soon as a human voice could make itself heard, the Governor called a slave.

"Run out to the place of execution and command in my name that the Prophet of Nazareth shall be taken down from the cross!"

The slave hurried away. The guests filed from the dining-hall out on the peristyle, to be under the open sky in case the earthquake should be repeated.

No one dared to utter a word, while they awaited the slave's return.

He came back very shortly. He stopped before the Governor.

"You found him alive?" said he.

"Master, he was dead, and on the very second that he gave up the ghost, the earthquake occurred."

The words were hardly spoken when two loud knocks sounded against the outer gate. When these knocks were heard, they all staggered back and leaped up, as though it had been a new earthquake.

Immediately afterwards a slave came up.

"It is the noble Faustina and the Emperor's kinsman Sulpicius. They are come to beg you help them find the Prophet from Nazareth."

A low murmur passed through the peristyle, and soft footfalls were heard. When the Governor looked around, he noticed that his friends had withdrawn from him, as from one upon whom misfortune has fallen.

IX

Old Faustina had returned to Capri and had sought out the Emperor. She told him her story, and while she spoke she hardly dared look at him. During her absence the illness had made frightful ravages, and she thought to herself: "If there had been any pity among the Celestials, they would have let me die before being forced to tell this poor, tortured man that all hope is gone."

To her astonishment, Tiberius listened to her with the utmost indifference. When she related how the great miracle-performer had been crucified the same day that she had arrived in Jerusalem, and how near she had been to saving him, she began to weep under the weight of her failure. But Tiberius only remarked: "You actually grieve over this? Ah, Faustina! A whole lifetime in Rome has not weaned you then of faith in sorcerers and miracle-workers, which you imbibed during your childhood in the Sabine mountains!"

Then the old woman perceived that Tiberius had never expected any help from the Prophet of Nazareth.

"Why did you let me make the journey to that distant land, if you believed all the while that it was useless?"

"You are the only friend I have," said the Emperor. "Why should I deny your prayer, so long as I still have the power to grant it."

But the old woman did not like it that the Emperor had taken her for a fool.

"Ah! this is your usual cunning," she burst out. "This is just what I can tolerate least in you."

"You should not have come back to me," said Tiberius. "You should have remained in the mountains."

It looked for a moment as if these two, who had clashed so often, would again fall into a war of words, but the old woman's anger subsided immediately. The times were past when she could quarrel in earnest with the Emperor. She lowered her voice again; but she could not altogether relinquish every effort to obtain justice.

"But this man was really a prophet," she said. "I have seen him. When his eyes met mine, I thought he was a god. I was mad to allow him to go to his death."

"I am glad you let him die," said Tiberius. "He was a traitor and a dangerous agitator."

Faustina was about to burst into another passion — then checked herself.

"I have spoken with many of his friends in Jerusalem about him," said she. "He had not committed the crimes for which he was arraigned."

"Even if he had not committed just these crimes, he was surely no better than anyone else," said the Emperor wearily. "Where will

133

you find the person who during his lifetime has not a thousand times deserved death?"

But these remarks of the Emperor decided Faustina to undertake something which she had until now hesitated about. "I will show you a proof of his power," said she. "I said to you just now that I laid my kerchief over his face. It is the same kerchief which I hold in my hand. Will you look at it a moment?"

She spread the kerchief out before the Emperor, and he saw delineated thereon the shadowy likeness of a human face.

The old woman's voice shook with emotion as she continued: "This man saw that I loved him. I know not by what power he was enabled to leave me his portrait. But mine eyes fill up with tears when I see it."

The Emperor leaned forward and regarded the picture, which appeared to be made up of blood and tears and the dark shadows of grief. Gradually the whole face stood out before him, exactly as it had been imprinted upon the kerchief. He saw the blood-drops on the forehead, the piercing thorn-crown, the hair, which was matted with blood, and the mouth whose lips seemed to quiver with agony.

He bent down closer and closer to the picture. The face stood out clearer and clearer. From out the shadow-like outlines, all at once, he saw the eyes sparkle as with hidden life. And while they spoke to him of the most terrible suffering, they also revealed a purity and sublimity which he had never seen before.

He lay upon his couch and drank in the picture with his eyes. "Is this a mortal?" he said softly and slowly. "Is this a mortal?"

Again he lay still and regarded the picture. The tears began to stream down his cheeks. "I mourn over thy death, thou Unknown!" he whispered.

"Faustina!" he cried out at last. "Why did you let this man die? He would have healed me."

134

And again he was lost in the picture.

"O Man!" he said, after a moment, "if I cannot gain my health from thee, I can still avenge thy murder. My hand shall rest heavily upon those who have robbed me of thee!"

Again he lay still a long time; then he let himself glide down to the floor — and he knelt before the picture:

"Thou art Man!" said he. "Thou art what I never dreamed I should see." And he pointed to his disfigured face and destroyed hands. "I and all others are wild beasts and monsters, but thou art Man."

He bowed his head so low before the picture that it touched the floor. "Have pity on me, thou Unknown!" he sobbed, and his tears watered the stones.

"If thou hadst lived, thy glance alone would have healed me," he said.

The poor old woman was terror-stricken over what she had done. It would have been wiser not to show the Emperor the picture, thought she. From the start she had been afraid that if he should see it his grief would be too overwhelming.

And in her despair over the Emperor's grief, she snatched the picture away, as if to remove it from his sight.

Then the Emperor looked up. And lo! his features were transformed, and he was as he had been before the illness. It was as if the illness had had its root and sustenance in the contempt and hatred of mankind which had lived in his heart; and it had been forced to flee the very moment he had felt love and compassion.

The following day Tiberius despatched three messengers.

The first messenger travelled to Rome with the command that the Senate should institute investigations as to how the governor of Palestine administered his official duties and punish him, should it appear that he oppressed the people and condemned the innocent to death.

135

The second messenger went to the vineyard-labourer and his wife, to thank them and reward them for the counsel they had given the Emperor, and also to tell them how everything had turned out. When they had heard all, they wept silently, and the man said: "I know that all my life I shall ponder what would have happened if these two had met." But the woman answered: "It could not happen in any other way. It was too great a thought that these two should meet. God knew that the world could not support it."

The third messenger travelled to Palestine and brought back with him to Capri some of Jesus's disciples, and these began to teach there the doctrine that had been preached by the Crucified One.

When the disciples landed at Capri, old Faustina lay upon her death-bed. Still they had time before her death to make of her a follower of the great Prophet, and to baptize her. And in the baptism she was called VERONICA, because to her it had been granted to give to mankind the true likeness of their Saviour.

Robin Redbreast

It happened at the time when Our Lord created the world, when He not only made heaven and earth, but all the animals and the plants as well, at the same time giving them their names.

There have been many histories concerning that time, and if we knew them all, we should have light upon everything in this world which we cannot now comprehend.

At that time it happened one day when Our Lord sat in His Paradise and painted the little birds, that the colours in Our Lord's paint pot gave out, and the goldfinch would have been without colour if Our Lord had not wiped all His paint brushes on its feathers.

It was then that the donkey got his long ears, because he could not remember the name that had been given him.

No sooner had he taken a few steps over the meadows of Paradise than he forgot, and three times he came back to ask his name. At last Our Lord grew somewhat impatient, took him by his two ears, and said:

"Thy name is ass, ass, ass!" And while He thus spake Our Lord pulled both of his ears that the ass might hear better, and remember what was said to him. It was on the same day, also, that the bee was punished.

Now, when the bee was created, she began immediately to gather honey, and the animals and human beings who caught the delicious odour of the honey came and wanted to taste of it. But the bee wanted to keep it all for herself and with her poisonous sting pursued every living creature that approached her hive. Our Lord saw this and at once called the bee to Him and punished her.

"I gave thee the gift of gathering honey, which is the sweetest thing in all creation," said Our Lord, "but I did not give thee the right to be cruel to thy neighbour. Remember well that every time thou stingest any creature who desires to taste of thy honey, thou shalt surely die!"

Ah, yes! It was at that time, too, that the cricket became blind and the ant missed her wings, so many strange things happened on that day!

Our Lord sat there, big and gentle, and planned and created all day long, and towards evening He conceived the idea of making a little grey bird. "Remember your name is Robin Redbreast," said Our Lord to the bird, as soon as it was finished. Then He held it in the palm of His open hand and let it fly.

After the bird had been testing his wings a while, and had seen something of the beautiful world in which he was destined to live, he became curious to see what he himself was like. He noticed that he was entirely grey, and that his breast was just as grey as all the rest of him. Robin Redbreast twisted and turned in all directions as he viewed himself in the mirror of a clear lake, but he couldn't find a single red feather. Then he flew back to Our Lord.

Our Lord sat there on His throne, big and gentle. Out of His hands came butterflies that fluttered about His head; doves cooed on His shoulders; and out of the earth beneath Him grew the rose, the lily, and the daisy.

The little bird's heart beat heavily with fright, but with easy curves he flew nearer and nearer Our Lord, till at last he rested on Our Lord's hand. Then Our Lord asked what the little bird wanted. "I only wish to ask you about one thing," said the little bird — "What is it you wish to know?" said Our Lord — "Why should I be called Redbreast, when I am all grey, from the bill to the very end of my tail? Why am I called Redbreast when I do not possess one single red feather?" The bird looked beseechingly on Our Lord with his tiny black eyes — then turned his head. About him he saw pheasants all red under a sprinkle of gold dust, parrots with marvellous red neckbands, cocks with red combs, to say nothing about the butterflies, the goldfinches, and the roses! And naturally he thought how little he needed — just one tiny drop of colour on his breast and he, too, would be a beautiful bird, and his name would fit him. "Why should I be called Redbreast when I am so entirely grey?" asked the bird once again, and waited for Our Lord to say: "Ah, my friend, I see that I have forgotten to paint your breast feathers red, but wait a moment and it shall be done."

But our Lord only smiled a little and said: "I have called you Robin Redbreast, and Robin Redbreast shall your name be, but you must look to it that you yourself earn your red breast feathers." Then Our Lord lifted His hand and let the bird fly once more — out into the world.

The bird flew down into Paradise, meditating deeply.

What could a little bird like him do to earn for himself red feathers? The only thing he could think of was to make his nest in a brier bush. He built it in among the thorns in the close thicket. It looked as if he waited for a rose leaf to cling to his throat and give him colour.

Countless years had come and gone since that day, which was the happiest in all the world. Human beings had already advanced so far that they had learned to cultivate the earth and sail the seas. They had procured clothes and ornaments for themselves, and had long since learned to build big temples and great cities — such as Thebes, Rome, and Jerusalem.

Then there dawned a *new* day, one that will long be remembered in the world's history. On the morning of this day Robin Redbreast sat upon a little naked hillock outside Jerusalem's walls, and sang to his young ones, who rested in a tiny nest in a brier bush.

Robin Redbreast told the little ones all about that wonderful day of creation, and how the Lord had given names to everything, just as each Redbreast had told it ever since the first Redbreast had heard God's word, and gone out of God's hand. "And mark you," he ended sorrowfully, "so many years have gone, so many roses have bloomed, so many little birds have come out of their eggs since Creation Day, but Robin Redbreast is still a little grey bird. He has not yet succeeded in gaining his red feathers."

The little ones opened wide their tiny bills, and asked if their forbears had never tried to do any great thing to earn the priceless red colour.

"We have all done what we could," said the little bird, "but we have all gone amiss. Even the first Robin Redbreast met one day another bird exactly like himself, and he began immediately to love it with such a mighty love that he could feel his breast burn. 'Ah!' he thought then, 'now I understand! It was Our Lord's meaning that I should love with so much ardour that my breast should grow red in colour from the very warmth of the love that lives in my heart.' But he missed it, as all those who came after him have missed it and as even you shall miss it."

The little ones twittered, utterly bewildered, and already began to mourn because the red colour would not come to beautify their little, downy grey breasts.

"We had also hoped that song would help us," said the grown-up bird, speaking in long, drawn-out tones, "the first Robin Redbreast sang until his heart swelled within him, he was so carried away, and he dared to hope anew. 'Ah!' he thought, 'it is the glow of the song

140

which lives in my soul that will colour my breast feathers red.' But he missed it, as all the others have missed it and as even you shall miss it." Again was heard a sad "peep" from the young ones' half-naked throats.

"We have also counted on our courage and our valour," said the bird. "The first Robin Redbreast fought bravely with other birds, until his breast flamed with the pride of conquest. 'Ah!' he thought, 'my breast feathers shall become red from the love of battle which burns in my heart.' He, too, missed it, as all those who came after him have missed it and as even you shall miss it." The little young ones peeped courageously that they still wished to try and win the much-sought-for prize, but the bird answered them sorrowfully that it would be impossible. What could they do when so many splendid ancestors had missed the mark? What could they do more than love, sing, and fight? What could — the little bird stopped short, for out of one of the gates of Jerusalem came a crowd of people marching, and the whole procession rushed toward the hillock, where the bird had its nest. There were riders on proud horses, soldiers with long spears, executioners with nails and hammers. There were judges and priests in the procession, weeping women, and above all a mob of mad, loose people running about — a filthy, howling mob of loiterers.

The little grey bird sat trembling on the edge of his nest. He feared each instant that the little brier bush would be trampled down and his young ones killed!

"Be careful!" he cried to the little defenceless young ones, "creep together and remain quiet. Here comes a horse that will ride right over us! Here comes a warrior with iron-shod sandals! Here comes the whole wild, storming mob!" Immediately the bird ceased his cry of warning and grew calm and quiet. He almost forgot the danger hovering over him. Finally he hopped down into the nest and spread his wings over the young ones.

"Oh! this is too terrible," said he. "I don't wish you to witness this awful sight. There are three miscreants who are going to be crucified!" And he spread his wings so that the little ones could see nothing.

They caught only the sound of hammers, the cries of anguish, and the wild shrieks of the mob.

Robin Redbreast followed the whole spectacle with his eyes, which grew big with terror. He could not take his glance from the three unfortunates.

"How terrible human beings are!" said the bird after a little while. "It isn't enought that they nail these poor creatures to a cross, but they must needs place a crown of piercing thorns upon the head of one of them. I see that the thorns have wounded his brow so that the blood flows," he continued. "And this man is so beautiful, and looks about him with such mild glances that every one ought to love him. I feel as if an arrow were shooting through my heart, when I see him suffer!"

The little bird began to feel a stronger and stronger pity for the thorn-crowned sufferer. "Oh! if I were only my brother the eagle," though he, "I would draw the nails from his hands, and with my strong claws I would drive away all those who torture him!" He saw how the blood trickled down from the brow of the Crucified One, and he could no longer remain quiet in his nest. "Even if I am little and weak, I can still do something for this poor tortured one," thought the bird. Then he left his nest and flew out into the air, striking wide circles around the Crucified One. He flew around him several times without daring to approach, for he was a shy little bird, who had never dared to go near a human being. But little by little he gained courage, flew close to him, and drew with his little bill a thorn that had become imbedded in the brow of the Crucified One. And as he did this there fell on his breast a drop of blood from the

143

face of the Crucified One; — it spread quickly and floated out and coloured all the little fine breast feathers.

Then the Crucified One opened his lips and whispered to the bird: "Because of thy compassion, thou hast won all that thy kind have been striving after, ever since the world was created."

As soon as the bird had returned to his nest his young ones cried to him: "Thy breast is red! Thy breast feathers are redder than the roses!"

"It is only a drop of blood from the poor man's forehead," said the bird; "it will vanish as soon as I bathe in a pool or a clear well."

But no matter how much the little bird bathed, the red colour did not vanish — and when his little young ones grew up, the blood-red colour shone also on their breast feathers, just as it shines on every Robin Redbreast's throat and breast until this very day.

The Bird's Nest

Hatto the hermit stood in the wilderness and prayed to God. A storm was raging, and his long beard and matted hair waved about him like weather-beaten tufts of grass on the summit of an old ruin. But he did not push his hair out of his eyes, not did he tuck his beard into his belt, for his arms were uplifted in prayer. Ever since sunrise he had raised his gnarled, hairy arms towards heaven, as untiringly as a tree stretches up its branches, and he meant to remain standing so till night. He had a great boon to pray for.

He was a man who had suffered much of the world's anger. He had himself persecuted and tortured, and persecutions and torture from others had fallen to his share, more than his heart could bear.

So he went out on the great heath, dug himself a hole in the river bank and became a holy man, whose prayers were heard at God's throne.

Hatto the hermit stood there on the river bank by his hole and prayed the great prayer of his life. He prayed to God that He should appoint the day of doom for this wicked world. He called on the trumpet-blowing angels, who were to proclaim the end of the reign of sin. He cried out to the waves of the sea of blood, which were to drown the unrighteous. He called on the pestilence, which should fill the churchyards with heaps of dead.

Round about stretched a desert plain. But a little higher up on the river bank stood an old willow with a short trunk, which swelled out at the top in a great knob like a head, from which new, light-green shoots grew out. Every autumn it was robbed of these strong, young branches by the inhabitants of that fuel-less heath. Every spring the tree put forth new, soft shoots, and in stormy weather these waved and fluttered about it, just as hair and beard fluttered about Hatto the hermit.

A pair of wagtails, which used to make their nest in the top of the willow's trunk among the sprouting branches, had intended to begin their building that very day. But among the whipping shoots the birds found no quiet. They came flying with straws and root-fibres and dried sedges, but they had to turn back with their errand unaccomplished. Just then they noticed old Hatto, who called upon God to make the storm seven times more violent, so that the nests of the little birds might be swept away and the eagle's eyrie destroyed.

Of course no one now living can conceive how mossy and dried-up and gnarled and black and unlike a human being such an old plain-dweller could be. The skin was so drawn over brow and cheeks, that he looked almost like a death's-head, and one saw only by a faint gleam in the hollows of the eye-sockets that he was alive.

And the dried-up muscles of the body gave it no roundness, and the upstretched, naked arms consisted only of shapeless bones, covered with shrivelled, hardened, bark-like skin. He wore an old, close-fitting, black robe. He was tanned by the sun and black with dirt. His hair and beard alone were light, bleached by the rain and sun, until they had become the same green-grey colour as the underside of the willow leaves.

The birds, flying about, looking for a place to build, took Hatto the hermit for another old willow-tree, checked in its struggle towards the sky by axe and saw like the first one. They circled about him many times, flew away and came again, took their landmarks, considered his position in regard to birds of prey and winds, found him rather unsatisfactory, but nevertheless decided in his favour, because he stood so near to the river and to the tufts of sedge, their larder and storehouse. One of them shot swift as an arrow down into his upstretched hand and laid his root-fibre there.

There was a lull in the storm, so that the root-fibre was not torn instantly away from the hand; but in the hermit's prayers there was no pause: "May the Lord come soon to destroy this world of corruption, so that man may not have time to heap more sin upon himself! May he save the unborn from life! For the living there is no salvation."

Then the storm began again, and the little root-fibre fluttered away out of the hermit's big gnarled hand. But the birds came again and tried to wedge the foundation of the new home in between the fingers. Suddenly a shapeless and dirty thumb laid itself on the straws and held them fast, and four fingers arched themselves so that there was a quiet niche to build in. The hermit continued his prayers.

"Oh Lord, where are the clouds of fire which laid Sodom waste? When wilt Thou let loose the floods which lifted the ark to Ararat's top? Are not the cups of Thy patience emptied and the vials of Thy

147

grace exhausted? Oh Lord, when wilt Thou rend the heavens and come?"

And feverish visions of the Day of Doom appeared to Hatto the hermit. The ground trembled, the heavens glowed. Across the flaming sky he saw black clouds of flying birds, a horde of panic-stricken beasts rushed, roaring and bellowing, past him. But while his soul was occupied with these fiery visions, his eyes began to follow the flight of the little birds, as they flashed to and fro and with a cheery peep of satisfaction wove a new straw into the nest.

The old man had no thought of moving. He had made a vow to pray without moving with uplifted hands all day in order to force the Lord to grant his request. The more exhausted his body became, the more vivid visions filled his brain. He heard the walls of cities fall and the houses crack. Shrieking, terrified crowds rushed by him, pursued by the angels of vengeance and destruction, mighty forms with stern, beautiful faces, wearing silver coats of mail, riding black horses and swinging scourges, woven of white lightning.

The little wagtails built and shaped busily all day, and the work progressed rapidly. On the tufted heath with its stiff sedges and by the river with its reeds and rushes, there was no lack of building material. They had no time for noon siesta nor for evening rest. Glowing with eagerness and delight, they flew to and fro, and before night came they had almost reached the roof.

But before night came, the hermit had begun to watch them more and more. He followed them on their journeys; he scolded them when they built foolishly; he was furious when the wind disturbed their work; and least of all could he endure that they should take any rest.

Then the sun set, and the birds went to their old sleeping-place in among the rushes.

Let him who crosses the heath at night bend down until his face

comes on a level with the tufts of grass, and he will see a strange spectacle outline itself against the western sky. Owls with great, round wings skim over the ground, invisible to anyone standing upright. Snakes glide about there, lithe, quick, with narrow heads uplifted on swan-like necks. Great turtles crawl slowly forward, hares and water-rats flee before preying beasts, and a fox bounds after a bat, which is chasing mosquitos by the river. It seems as if every tuft has come to life. But through it all the little birds sleep on the waving rushes, secure from all harm in that resting-place which no enemy can approach, without the water splashing or the reeds shaking and waking them.

When the morning came, the wagtails believed at first that the events of the day before had been a beautiful dream.

They had taken their landmarks and flew straight to their nest, but it was gone. They flew searching over the heath and rose up into the air to spy about. There was not a trace of nest or tree. At last they lighted on a couple of stones by the river bank and considered. They wagged their long tails and cocked their heads on one side. Where had the tree and nest gone?

But hardly had the sun risen a handsbreadth over the belt of trees on the other bank, before their tree came walking and placed itself on the same spot where it had been the day before. It was just as black and gnarled as ever and bore their nest on the top of something, which must be a dry, upright branch.

Then the wagtails began to build again, without troubling themselves any more about Nature's many wonders.

Hatto the hermit, who drove the little children away from his hole telling them that it had been best for them if they had never been born, he who rushed out into the mud to hurl curses after the joyous young people who rowed up the stream in pleasure-boats, he from whose angry eyes the shepherds on the heath guarded their flocks, did not return to his place by the river for the sake of the little birds. He knew that not only has every letter in the holy books its hidden, mysterious meaning, but so also has everything which God allows to take place in Nature. He had thought out the meaning of the wagtails building in his hand. God wished him to remain standing with uplifted arms until the birds had raised their brood; and if he should have the power to do that, he would be heard.

But during that day he did not see so many visions of the Day of Doom. Instead, he watched the birds more and more eagerly. He saw the nest soon finished. The little builders fluttered about it and inspected it. They went after a few bits of lichen from the real willow-tree and fastened them on the outside, to fill the place of plaster and paint. They brought the finest cotton-grass, and the female wagtail took feathers from her own breast and lined the nest.

The peasants, who feared the baleful power that the hermit's prayers might have at the throne of God, used to bring him bread and milk to mitigate his wrath. They came now too and found him standing motionless, with the bird's nest in his hand. "See how the holy man loves the little creatures," they said, and were no longer afraid of him, but lifted the bowl of milk to his mouth and put the bread between his lips. When he had eaten and drunk, he drove away the people with angry words, but they only smiled at his curses.

His body had long since become the slave of his will. By hunger and blows, by praying all day, by waking a week at a time, he had taught it obedience. Now the steel-like muscles held his arms uplifted for days and weeks, and when the female wagtail began to sit on her eggs and never left the nest, he did not return to his hole even at night. He learned to sleep sitting, with upstretched arms. Among the dwellers in the wilderness there are many who have done greater things.

151

He grew accustomed to the two little, motionless bird-eyes which stared down at him over the edge of the nest. He watched for hail and rain, and sheltered the nest as well as he could.

At last one day the female was freed from her duties. Both the birds sat on the edge of the nest, wagged their tails and consulted and looked delighted, although the whole nest seemed to be full of an anxious peeping. Then they set out on the wildest hunt for midges.

Midge after midge was caught and brought to whatever it was that was peeping up there in his hand. And when the food came, the peeping was at its very loudest. The holy man was disturbed in his prayers by that peeping.

And gently, gently he bent his arm, which had almost lost the power of moving, and his little fiery eyes stared down into the nest.

Never had he seen anything so helplessly ugly and miserable: small, naked bodies, with a little thin down, no eyes, no power of flight, nothing really but six big, gaping mouths.

It seemed very strange to him, but he liked them just as they were. Their father and mother he had never spared in the general destruction, but when hereafter he called to God to ask Him the salvation of the world through its annihilation, he made a silent exception of those six helpless ones.

When the peasant women now brought him food, he no longer thanked them by wishing their destruction. Since he was necessary to the little creatures up there, he was glad that they did not let him starve to death.

Soon six round heads were to be seen the whole day long stretching over the edge of the nest. Old Hatto's arm sank more and more often to the level of his eyes. He saw the feathers push out through the red skin, the eyes open, the bodies round out. Happy inheritors of the beauty Nature has given to flying creatures, they developed quickly in their loveliness.

And during all this time prayers for the great destruction rose more and more hesitatingly to old Hatto's lips. He thought that he had God's promise, that it should come when the little birds were fledged. Now he seemed to be searching for a loop-hole for God the Father. For these six little creatures, whom he had sheltered and cherished, he could not sacrifice.

It was another matter before, when he had not had anything that was his own. The love for the small and weak — which it has been every little child's mission to teach big, dangerous people — came over him and made him doubtful.

He sometimes wanted to hurl the whole nest into the river, for he thought that they who die without sorrow or sin are the happy ones. Should he not save them from beasts of prey and cold, from hunger, and from life's manifold visitations? But just as he thought this, a sparrow-hawk came swooping down on the nest. Then Hatto seized the marauder with his left hand, swung him about his head and hurled him with the strength of wrath out into the stream.

The day came at last when the little birds were ready to fly. One of the wagtails was working inside the nest to push the young ones out to the edge, while the other flew about, showing them how easy it was, if they only dared to try. And when the young ones were obstinate and afraid, both the parents flew about, showing them all their most beautiful feats of flight. Beating with their wings, they flew in swooping curves, or rose right up like larks or hung motionless in the air with vibrating wings.

But as the young ones still persisted in their obstinacy, Hatto the hermit could not keep from mixing himself up in the matter. He gave them a cautious shove with his finger and then it was done. Out they went, fluttering and uncertain, beating the air like bats, sinking, but rising again, grasping what the art is and making use of it to reach the nest again as quickly as possible. Proud and rejoicing, the parents came to them again and old Hatto smiled. It was he who gave the final touch after all.

He now considered seriously if there could not be any way out of it for Our Lord.

Perhaps, when all was said, God the Father held this earth in His right hand like a big bird's nest, and perhaps He had come to cherish love for all those who build and dwell there, for all earth's defence-less children. Perhaps He felt pity for those whom He had promised to destroy, just as the hermit felt pity for the little birds.

Of course the hermit's birds were much better than Our Lord's people, but he could quite understand that God the Father neverthe-less had love for them.

The next day the bird's nest stood empty, and the bitterness of loneliness filled the heart of the hermit. Slowly his arm sank down to his side, and it seemed to him as if all nature held its breath to listen for the thunder of the trumpet of Doom. But just then all the wagtails came again and lighted on his head and shoulders, for they were not at all afraid of him. Then a ray of light shot through old Hatto's confused brain. He had lowered his arm, lowered it every day to look at the birds.

And standing there with all the six young ones fluttering and playing about him, he nodded contentedly to someone whom he did not see. "I let you off," he said, "I let you off. I have not kept my word, so you need not keep yours."

And it seemed to him as if the mountains ceased to tremble and as if the river laid itself down in easy calm in its bed.

The Christmas Rose

Robber Mother, who lived in Robbers' Cave up in Göinge Forest, went down to the village one day on a begging tour. Robber Father, who was an outlawed man, did not dare to leave the forest. She took with her five youngsters, and each youngster bore a sack on his back as long as himself. When Robber Mother stepped inside the door of a cabin, no one dared refuse to give her whatever she demanded; for she was not above coming back the following night and setting fire to the house if she had not been well received. Robber Mother and her brood were worse than a pack of wolves, and many a man felt like running a spear through them; but it was never done, because they all knew that the man stayed up in the forest, and he would have known how to wreak vengeance if anything had happened to the children or the old woman.

Now that Robber Mother went from house to house and begged, she came to Övid, which at that time was a cloister. She rang the bell of the cloister gate and asked for food. The watchman let down a small wicket in the gate and handed her six round bread cakes — one for herself and one for each of the five children.

While the mother was standing quietly at the gate, her youngsters were running about. And now one of them came and pulled at her skirt, as a signal that he had discovered something which she ought to come and see, and Robber Mother followed him promptly.

The entire cloister was surrounded by a high and strong wall, but the youngster had managed to find a little back gate which stood

155

ajar. When Robber Mother got there, she pushed the gate open and walked inside without asking leave, as it was her custom to do.

Övid Cloister was managed at that time by Abbot Hans, who knew all about herbs. Just within the cloister wall he had planted a little herb garden, and it was into this that the old woman had forced her way.

At first glance Robber Mother was so astonished that she paused at the gate. It was high summer-tide, and Abbot Hans' garden was so full of flowers that the eyes were fairly dazzled by the blues, reds, and yellows, as one looked into it. But presently an indulgent smile spread over her features, and she started to walk up a narrow path that lay between many flower-beds.

In the garden a lay brother walked about, pulling up weeds. It was he who had left the door in the wall open, that he might throw the weeds and tares on the rubbish-heap outside.

When he saw Robber Mother coming in, with all five youngsters in tow, he ran towards her at once and ordered them away. But the beggar woman walked right on as before. The lay brother knew of no other remedy than to run into the cloister and call for help.

He returned with two stalwart monks, and Robber Mother saw that now it meant business! She let out a perfect volley of shrieks, and, throwing herself upon the monks, clawed and bit at them; so did all the youngsters. The men soon learned that she could over-power them, and all they could do was to go back into the cloister for reinforcements.

As they ran through the passage-way which led to the cloister, they met Abbot Hans, who came rushing out to learn what all this noise was about.

He upbraided them for using force and forbade their calling for help. He sent both monks back to their work, and although he was an old and fragile man, he took with him only the lay brother.

156

He came up to the woman and asked in a mild tone if the garden pleased her.

Robber Mother turned defiantly towards Abbot Hans, for she expected only to be trapped and overpowered. But when she noticed his white hair and bent form, she answered peaceably: "First, when I saw this, I thought I had never seen a prettier garden; but now I see that it can't be compared with one I know of. If you could see the garden of which I am thinking you would uproot all the flowers planted there and cast them away like weeds."

The Abbot's assistant was hardly less proud of the flowers than the Abbot himself, and after hearing her remarks he laughed derisively.

Robber Mother grew crimson with rage to think that her word was doubted, and she cried out: "You monks, who are holy men, certainly must know that on every Christmas Eve the great Göinge Forest is transformed into a beautiful garden, to commemorate the hour of Our Lord's birth. We who live in the forest have seen this happen every year. And in that garden I have seen flowers so lovely that I dared not lift my hand to pluck them."

Ever since his childhood, Abbot Hans had heard it said that on every Christmas Eve the forest was dressed in holiday glory. He had often longed to see it, but he had never had the good fortune. Eagerly he begged and implored Robber Mother that he might come up to the Robbers' Cave on Christmas Eve. If she would only send one of her children to show him the way, he could ride up there alone, and he would never betray them — on the contrary, he would reward them in so far as it lay in his power.

Robber Mother said no at first, for she was thinking of Robber Father and of the peril which might befall him should she permit Abbot Hans to ride up to their cave. At the same time the desire to prove to the monk that the garden which she knew was more beautiful than his got the better of her, and she gave in.

157

"But more than one follower you cannot take with you," said she, "and you are not to waylay us or trap us, as sure as you are a holy man."

This Abbot Hans promised, and then Robber Mother went her way.

It happened that Archbishop Absalon from Lund came to Övid and remained through the night. The lay brother heard Abbot Hans telling the Bishop about Robber Father and asking him for a letter of ransom for the man, that he might lead an honest life among respectable folk.

But the Archbishop replied that he did not care to let the robber loose among honest folk in the villages. It would be best for all that he remained in the forest.

Then Abbot Hans grew zealous and told the Bishop all about Göinge Forest, which, every year at Yuletide, clothed itself in summer bloom around the Robbers' Cave. "If these bandits are not so bad but that God's Glories can be made manifest to them, surely we cannot be too wicked to experience the same blessing."

The Archbishop knew how to answer Abbot Hans. "This much I will promise you, Abbot Hans," he said, smiling, "that any day you send me a blossom from the garden of Göinge Forest, I will give you letters of ransom for all the outlaws you may choose to plead for."

The following Christmas Eve Abbot Hans was on his way to the forest. One of Robber Mother's wild youngsters ran ahead of him, and close behind him was the lay brother.

It turned out to be a long and hazardous ride. They climbed steep and slippery side paths, crawled over swamp and marsh, and pushed through windfall and bramble. Just as daylight was waning, the robber boy guided them across a forest meadow, skirted by tall, naked leaf trees and green fir trees. Behind the meadow loomed a mountain wall, and in this wall they saw a door of thick boards. Now

Abbot Hans understood that they had arrived, and dismounted. The child opened the heavy door for him, and he looked into a poor mountain grotto, with bare stone walls. Robber Mother was seated before a log fire that burned in the middle of the floor. Alongside the walls were beds of virgin pine and moss, and on one of these beds lay Robber Father asleep.

"Come in, you out there!" shouted Robber Mother, without rising, "and fetch the horses in with you, so they won't be destroyed by the night cold."

Abbot Hans walked boldly into the cave, and the lay brother followed. Here were wretchedness and poverty, and nothing was done to celebrate Christmas.

Robber Mother spoke in a tone as haughty and dictatorial as any well-to-do peasant woman. "Sit down by the fire and warm yourself, Abbot Hans," said she; "and if you have food with you, eat, for the food which we in the forest prepare you wouldn't care to taste. And if you are tired after the long journey, you can lie down on one of these beds to sleep. You needn't be afraid of oversleeping, for I'm sitting here by the fire keeping watch. I shall awaken you in time to see what you have come up here to see."

Abbot Hans obeyed Robber Mother and brought forth his foodsack; but he was so fatigued after the journey he was hardly able to eat, and as soon as he could stretch himself on the bed, he fell asleep.

The lay brother was also assigned a bed to rest and he dropped into a doze.

When he woke up, he saw that Abbot Hans had left his bed and was sitting by the fire talking with Robber Mother. The outlawed robber sat also by the fire. He was a tall, raw-boned man with a dull, sluggish appearance. His back was turned to Abbot Hans, as though he would have it appear that he was not listening to the conversation.

159

Abbot Hans was telling Robber Mother all about the Christmas preparations he had seen on the journey, reminding her of Christmas feasts and games which she must have known in her youth, when she lived at peace with mankind.

At first Robber Mother answered in short, gruff sentences, but by degrees she became more subdued and listened more intently. Suddenly Robber Father turned towards Abbot Hans and shook his clenched fist in his face. "You miserable monk! did you come here to coax from me my wife and children? Don't you know that I am an outlaw and may not leave the forest?"

Abbot Hans looked him fearlessly in the eyes. "It is my purpose to get a letter of ransom for you from Archbishop Absalon," said he. He had hardly finished speaking when the robber and his wife burst out laughing. They knew well enough the kind of mercy a forest robber could expect from Bishop Absalon!

"Oh, if I get a letter of ransom from Absalon!" said Robber Father, "then I'll promise you that never again will I steal so much as a goose."

Suddenly Robber Mother rose. "You sit here and talk, Abbot Hans," she said, "so that we are forgetting to look at the forest. Now I can hear, even in this cave, how the Christmas bells are ringing."

The words were barely uttered when they all sprang up and rushed out. But in the forest it was still dark night and bleak winter. The only thing they marked was a distant clank borne on a light south wind.

When the bells had been ringing a few moments, a sudden illumination penetrated the forest; the next moment it was dark again, and then light came back. It pushed its way forward between the stark trees, like a shimmering mist. The darkness merged into a faint daybreak. Then Abbot Hans saw that the snow had vanished from the ground, as if someone had removed a carpet, and the earth began to take on a green covering. The moss-tufts thickened and raised themselves, and the spring blossoms shot upward their swelling buds, which already had a touch of colour.

Again it grew hazy; but almost immediately there came a new wave of light. Then the leaves of the trees burst into bloom, crossbeaks hopped from branch to branch, and the woodpeckers hammered on the limbs until the splinters fairly flew around them. A flock of starlings from up-country lighted in a fir top to rest.

When the next warm wind came along, the blueberries ripened and the baby squirrels began playing on the branches of the trees.

The next light wave that came rushing in brought with it the scent of newly ploughed acres. Pine and spruce trees were so thickly clothed with red cones that they shone like crimson mantles and forest flowers covered the ground till it was all red, blue, and yellow.

Abbot Hans bent down to the earth and broke off a wild strawberry blossom, and, as he straightened up, the berry ripened in his hand.

The mother fox came out of her lair with a big litter of black-legged young. She went up to Robber Mother and scratched at her skirt, and Robber Mother bent down to her and praised her young.

Robber Mother's youngsters let out perfect shrieks of delight. They stuffed themselves with wild strawberries that hung on the bushes. One of them played with a litter of young hares; another ran a race with some young crows, which had hopped from their nest before they were really ready.

Robber Father was standing out on a marsh eating raspberries. When he glanced up, a big black bear stood beside him. Robber Father broke off a twig and struck the bear on the nose. "Keep to your own ground, you!" he said; "this is my turf." The huge bear turned around and lumbered off in another direction.

Then all the flowers whose seeds have been brought from foreign

L

lands began to blossom. The loveliest roses climbed up the mountain wall in a race with the blackberry vines, and from the forest meadow sprang flowers as large as human faces.

Abbot Hans thought of the flower he was to pluck for Bishop Absalon; but each new flower that appeared was more beautiful than the others, and he wanted to choose the most beautiful of all.

Then Abbot Hans marked how all grew still; the birds hushed their songs, the flowers ceased growing, and the young foxes played no more. From far in the distance faint harp tones were heard, and celestial song, like a soft murmur, reached him.

He clasped his hands and dropped to his knees. His face was radiant with bliss.

But beside Abbot Hans stood the lay brother who had accompanied him. In his mind there were dark thoughts. "This cannot be a true miracle," he thought, "since it is revealed to malefactors. This does not come from God, but is sent hither by Satan. It is the Evil One's power that is tempting us and compelling us to see that which has no real existence."

The angel throng was so near now that Abbot Hans saw their bright forms through the forest branches. The lay brother saw them, too; but behind all this wondrous beauty he saw only some dread evil.

All the while the birds had been circling around the head of Abbot Hans, and they let him take them in his hands. But all the animals were afraid of the lay brother; no bird perched on his shoulder, no snake played at his feet. Then there came a little forest dove. When she marked that the angels were nearing, she plucked up courage and flew down on the lay brother's shoulder and laid her head against his cheek.

Then it appeared to him as if sorcery were come right upon him, to tempt and corrupt him. He struck with his hand at the forest dove

and cried in such a loud voice that it rang throughout the forest: "Go thou back to hell, whence thou art come!"

Just then the angels were so near that Abbot Hans felt the feathery touch of their great wings, and he bowed down to earth in reverent greeting.

But when the lay brother's words sounded, their song was hushed and the holy guests turned in flight. At the same time the light and the mild warmth vanished in unspeakable terror for the darkness and cold in a human heart. Darkness sank over the earth, like a coverlet; frost came, all the growths shrivelled up; the animals and birds hastened away; the leaves dropped from the trees, rustling like rain.

Abbot Hans felt how his heart, which had but lately swelled with bliss, was now contracting with insufferable agony. "I can never outlive this," thought he, "that the angels from heaven had been so close to me and were driven away; that they wanted to sing Christmas carols for me and were driven to flight."

Then he remembered the flower he had promised Bishop Absalon, and at the last moment he fumbled among the leaves and moss to try and find a blossom. But he sensed how the ground under his fingers froze and how the white snow came gliding over the ground. Then his heart caused him even greater anguish. He could not rise, but fell prostrate on the ground and lay there.

When the robber folk and the lay brother had groped their way back to the cave, they missed Abbot Hans. They took brands with them and went out to search for him. They found him dead upon the coverlet of snow.

When Abbot Hans had been carried down to Övid, those who took charge of the dead saw that he held his right hand locked tight around something which he must have grasped at the moment of death. When they finally got his hand open, they found that the thing which he had held in such an iron grip was a pair of white root bulbs, which he had torn from among the moss and leaves.

When the lay brother who had accompanied Abbot Hans saw the bulbs, he took them and planted them in Abbot Hans' herb garden.

He guarded them the whole year to see if any flower would spring from them. But in vain he waited through the spring, the summer, and the autumn. Finally, when winter had set in and all the leaves and the flowers were dead, he ceased caring for them.

But when Christmas Eve came again, he was so strongly reminded of Abbot Hans that he wandered out into the garden to think of him. And look! as he came to the spot where he had planted the bare root bulbs, he saw that from them had sprung flourishing green stalks, which bore beautiful flowers with silver leaves.

He called out all the monks at Övid, and when they saw that this plant bloomed on Christmas Eve, when all the other growths were as if dead, they understood that this flower had in truth been plucked by Abbot Hans from the Christmas garden in Göinge Forest. Then the lay brother asked the monks if he might take a few blossoms to Bishop Absalon.

When Bishop Absalon beheld the flowers, which had sprung from the earth in darkest winter, he turned as pale as if he had met a ghost. He sat in silence a moment; thereupon he said: "Abbot Hans has faithfully kept his word and I shall also keep mine."

He handed the letter of ransom to the lay brother, who departed at once for the Robbers' Cave. When he stepped in there on Christmas Day, the robber came towards him with an axe uplifted. "I'd like to hack you monks into bits, as many as you are!" said he. "It must be your fault that Göinge Forest did not last night dress itself in Christmas bloom."

"The fault is mine alone," said the lay brother, "and I will gladly die for it; but first I must deliver a message from Abbot Hans." And

165

he drew forth the Bishop's letter and told the man that he was free.

Robber Father stood there pale and speechless, but Robber Mother said in his name: "Abbot Hans has indeed kept his word, and Robber Father will keep his."

When the Robber and his wife left the cave, the lay brother moved in and lived all alone in the forest, in constant meditation and prayer that his hard-heartedness might be forgiven him.

But Göinge Forest never again celebrated the hour of our Saviour's birth; and of all its glory, there lives today only the plant which Abbot Hans had plucked. It has been named CHRISTMAS ROSE. And each year at Christmastide she sends forth from the earth her green stalks and white blossoms, as if she never could forget that she had once grown in the great Christmas garden at Göinge Forest.

The Sacred Flame

A great many years ago, when the city of Florence had only just been made a republic, a man lived there named Raniero di Raniero. He was the son of an armourer, and had learned his father's trade, but he did not care much to pursue it.

This Raniero was the strongest of men. It was said of him that he bore a heavy iron armour as lightly as others wear a silk shirt. He was still a young man, but already he had given many proofs of his strength. Once he was in a house where grain was stored in the loft. Too much grain had been heaped there; and while Raniero was in the house one of the loft beams broke down, and the whole roof was about to fall in. He raised his arms and held the roof up until the people managed to fetch beams and poles to prop it.

It was also said of Raniero that he was the bravest man that had ever lived in Florence, and that he could never get enough of fighting. As soon as he heard any noise in the street, he rushed out from the workshop, in hopes that a fight had arisen in which he might participate. If he could only distinguish himself, he fought just as readily with humble peasants as with armoured horsemen. He rushed into a fight like a lunatic, without counting his opponents.

Florence was not very powerful in his time. The people were mostly wool spinners and cloth weavers, and these asked nothing better than to be allowed to perform their tasks in peace. Sturdy men were plentiful, but they were not quarrelsome, and they were proud of the fact that in their city better order prevailed than elsewhere. Raniero often grumbled because he was not born in a country where there was a king who gathered around him valiant men, and declared that in such an event he would have attained great honour and renown.

Raniero was loud-mouthed and boastful; cruel to animals, harsh toward his wife, and not good for any one to live with. He would have been handsome if he had not had several deep scars across his face which disfigured him. He was quick to jump to conclusions, and quick to act, though his way was often violent.

Raniero was married to Francesca, who was the daughter of Jacopo degli Uberti, a wise and influential man. Jacopo had not been very anxious to give his daughter to such a bully as Raniero and had opposed the marriage until the very last. Francesca forced him to relent, by declaring that she would never marry anyone else. When Jacopo finally gave his consent, he said to Raniero: "I have observed that men like you can more easily win a woman's love than keep it; therefore I shall exact this promise from you: If my daughter finds life with you so hard that she wishes to come back to me, you will not prevent her." Francesca said it was needless to exact such a promise, since she was so fond of Raniero that nothing could separate her from him. But Raniero gave his promise promptly. "Of one thing you can be assured, Jacopo," said he, "I will not try to hold any woman who wishes to flee from me."

Then Francesca went to live with Raniero, and all was well between them for a time. When they had been married a few weeks, Raniero took it into his head that he would practise marksmanship. For several days he aimed at a painting which hung upon a wall. He soon became skilled, and hit the mark every time. At last he thought he would like to try and shoot at a more difficult mark. He looked around for something suitable, but discovered nothing except a quail that sat in a cage above the courtyard gate. The bird belonged to Francesca, and she was very fond of it; but, despite this, Raniero sent a page to open the cage, and shot the quail as it swung itself into the air.

This seemed to him a very good shot, and he boasted of it to anyone who would listen to him.

When Francesca learned that Raniero had shot her bird, she grew pale and looked hard at him. She marvelled that he had wished to do a thing which must bring grief to her; but she forgave him promptly and loved him as before.

Then all went well again for a time.

Raniero's father-in law, Jacopo, was a flax weaver. He had a large establishment, where much work was done. Raniero thought he had discovered that hemp was mixed with the flax in Jacopo's workshop, and he did not keep silent about it, but talked of it here and there in the city. At last Jacopo also heard this chatter, and tried at once to put a stop to it. He let several other flax weavers examine his yarn, and cloth, and they found all of it to be of the very finest flax. Only in one pack, which was designed to be sold outside Florence, was there any mixture. Then Jacopo said that the deception had been practised without his knowledge or consent, by someone among his journeymen. He apprehended at once that he would find it difficult to convince people of this. He had always been famed for honesty, and he felt very keenly that his honour has been smirched.

Raniero, on the other hand, plumed himself upon having succeeded in exposing a fraud, and he bragged about it even in Francesca's hearing.

She felt deeply grieved; at the same time she was astonished as when he shot the bird. As she thought of this, she seemed suddenly to see her love before her; and it was like a great piece of shimmery gold cloth. She could see how big it was, and how it shimmered. But from one corner a piece had been cut away, so that it was not as big and as beautiful as it had been in the beginning.

Still, it was as yet damaged so very little that she thought: "It will probably last as long as I live. It as so great that it can never come to an end."

Again, there was a period during which she and Raniero were just as happy as they had been at first.

Francesca had a brother named Taddeo. He had been in Venice on a business trip, and, while there, had purchased garments of silk and velvet. When he came home he paraded around in them. Now, in Florence it was not the custom to go about expensively clad, so there were many who made fun of him.

One night Taddeo and Raniero were out in the wine shops. Taddeo was dressed in a green cloak with sable linings, and a violet jacket. Raniero tempted him to drink so much wine that he fell asleep, and then he took his cloak off him and hung it upon a scarecrow that was set up in a cabbage patch.

When Francesca heard of this she was vexed again with Raniero. That moment she saw before her the big piece of gold cloth — which was her love — and she seemed to see how it diminished, as Raniero cut away piece after piece.

After this, things were patched up between them for a time, but Francesca was no longer so happy as in former days, because she always feared that Raniero would commit some misdemeanour that would hurt her love.

This was not long in coming, either, for Raniero could never be tranquil. He wished that people should always speak of him and praise his courage and daring.

At that time the cathedral in Florence was much smaller than the present one, and there hung at the top of one of its towers a big, heavy shield, which had been placed there by one of Francesca's ancestors. It was the heaviest shield any man in Florence had been able to lift, and all the Uberti family were proud because it was one of their own who had climbed up in the tower and hung it there.

But Raniero climbed up to the shield one day, hung it on his back, and came down with it.

When Francesca heard of this for the first time she spoke to Raniero of what troubled her, and begged him not to humiliate her family in this way. Raniero, who had expected that she would commend him for his feat, became very angry. He retorted that he had long observed that she did not rejoice in his success, but thought only of her own kin. "It's something else I am thinking of," said Francesca, "and that is my love. I know not what will become of it if you keep on in this way."

After this they frequently exchanged harsh words, for Raniero happened nearly always to do the very thing that was most distasteful to Francesca.

There was a workman in Raniero's shop who was little and lame. This man had loved Francesca before she was married, and continued to love her even after her marriage. Raniero, who knew this, undertook to joke with him before all who sat at a table. It went so far that finally the man could no longer bear to be held up to ridicule in Francesca's hearing, so he rushed upon Raniero and wanted to fight with him. But Raniero only smiled derisively and kicked him aside. Then the poor fellow thought he did not care to live any longer, and went off and hanged himself.

When this happened, Francesca and Raniero had been married about a year. Francesca thought continually that she saw her love before her as a shimmery piece of cloth, but on all sides large pieces were cut away, so that it was scarcely half as big as it had been in the beginning.

171

She became very much alarmed when she saw this, and thought: "If I stay with Raniero another year, he will destroy my love. I shall become just as poor as I have hitherto been rich."

Then she decided to leave Raniero's house and go to live with her father, that the day might not come when she should hate Raniero as much as she now loved him.

Jacopo degli Uberti was sitting at the loom with all his workmen busy around him when he saw her coming. He said that now the thing had come to pass which he had long expected, and bade her be welcome. Instantly he ordered all the people to leave off their work and arm themselves and close the house.

Then Jacopo went over to Raniero. He met him in the workshop. "My daughter has this day returned to me and begged that she may live again under my roof," he said to his son-in-law. "And now I expect that you will not compel her to return to you, after the promise you have given me."

Raniero did not seem to take this very seriously, but answered calmly: "Even if I had not given you my word, I would not demand the return of a woman who does not wish to be mine."

He knew how much Francesca loved him, and said to himself: "She will be back with me before evening."

Yet she did not appear either that day or the next.

The third day Raniero went out and pursued a couple of robbers who had long disturbed the Florentine merchants. He succeeded in catching them, and took them captives to Florence.

He remained quiet a couple of days, until he was positive that this feat was known throughout the city. But it did not turn out as he had expected — that it would bring Francesca back to him.

Raniero had the greatest desire to appeal to the courts, to force her return to him, but he felt himself unable to do this because of his promise. It seemed impossible for him to live in the same city with a wife who had abandoned him, so he moved away from Florence.

He first became a soldier, and very soon he made himself commander of a volunteer company. He was always in a fight, and served many masters.

He won much renown as a warrior, as he had always said he would. He was made a knight by the Emperor, and was accounted a great man.

Before he left Florence, he had made a vow at a sacred image of the Madonna in the Cathedral to present to the Blessed Virgin the best and rarest that he won in every battle. Before this image one always saw costly gifts, which were presented by Raniero.

Raniero was aware that all his deeds were known in his native city. He marvelled much that Francesca degli Uberti did not come back to him, when she knew all about his success.

At that time sermons were preached to start the Crusades for the recovery of the Holy Sepulchre from the Saracens, and Raniero took the cross and departed for the Orient. He not only hoped to win castles and lands to rule over, but also to succeed in performing such brilliant feats that his wife would again be fond of him, and return to him.

II

The night succeeding the day on which Jerusalem had been captured, there was great rejoicing in the Crusaders' camp, outside the city. In almost every tent they celebrated with drinking bouts, and noise and roystering were heard in every direction.

Raniero di Raniero sat and drank with some comrades; and in his tent it was even more hilarious than elsewhere. The servants barely had time to fill the goblets before they were empty again.

Raniero had the best of reasons for celebrating because during the day he had won greater glory than ever before. In the morning, when the city was besieged, he had been the first to scale the walls after Godfrey of Boulogne; and in the evening he had been honoured for his bravery in the presence of the whole corps.

When the plunder and murder were ended, and the Crusaders in penitents' cloaks and with lighted candles marched into the Church of the Holy Sepulchre, it had been announced to Raniero by Godfrey that he should be the first who might light his candle from the sacred candles which burn before Christ's tomb. It appeared to Raniero that Godfrey wished in this manner to show that he considered him the bravest man in the whole corps; and he was very happy over the way in which he had been rewarded for his achievements.

As the night wore on, Raniero and his guests were in the best of spirits; a fool and a couple of musicians who had wandered all over the camp and amused the people with their pranks, came into Raniero's tent, and the fool asked permission to narrate a comic story.

Raniero knew that this particular fool was in great demand for his drollery, and he promised to listen to his narrative.

"It happened once," said the fool, "that Our Lord and Saint Peter sat a whole day upon the highest tower in Paradise Stronghold, and looked down upon the earth. They had so much to look at, that they scarcely found time to exchange a word. Our Lord kept perfectly still the whole time, but Saint Peter sometimes clapped his hands for joy, and again turned his head away in disgust. Sometimes he applauded and smiled, and anon he wept and commiserated. Finally, as it drew toward the close of day, and twilight sank down over Paradise, Our Lord turned to Saint Peter and said that now he must surely be satisfied and content. 'What is it that I should be content with?' Saint Peter asked, in an impetuous tone — 'Why,' said Our Lord slowly, 'I thought that you would be pleased with what you have seen today.' But Saint Peter did not care to be conciliated — 'It is true', said he, 'that for many years I have bemoaned the fact that Jerusalem should be in the power of unbelievers, but after all that has happened today, I think it might just as well have remained as it was'."

Raniero understood now that the fool spoke of what had taken place during the day. Both he and the other knights began to listen with greater interest than in the beginning.

"When Saint Peter had said this," continued the fool, as he cast a furtive glance at the knights, "he leaned over the pinnacle of the tower and pointed toward the earth. He showed Our Lord a city which lay upon a great solitary rock that shot up from a mountain valley. 'Do you see those mounds of corpses?' he said. 'And do you see the naked and wretched prisoners who moan in the night chill? And do you see all the smoking ruins of the conflagration?' It appeared as if Our Lord did not wish to answer him, but Saint Peter went on with his lamentations. He said that he had certainly been vexed with that city many times, but he had not wished it so ill as that it should come to look like this. Then, at last, Our Lord answered, and tried an objection: 'Still, you cannot deny that the Christian knights have risked their lives with the utmost fearlessness,' said He."

Then the fool was interrupted by bravos, but he made haste to continue.

"Oh, don't interrupt me!" he said. "Now I don't remember where I left off — ah! to be sure, I was just going to say that Saint Peter wiped away a tear or two which sprang to his eyes and prevented him from seeing. 'I never would have thought they could be such beasts,' said he. 'They have murdered and plundered the whole day. Why you went to all the trouble of letting yourself be crucified in order to gain such devotees, I can't in the least comprehend.' "

The knights took up the fun good-naturedly. They began to laugh loud and merrily. "What, fool! Is Saint Peter so wroth with us?" shrieked one of them.

"Be silent now, and let us hear if Our Lord spoke in our defence!" interposed another.

"No, Our Lord was silent. He knew of old that when Saint Peter had once got a-going, it wasn't worth while to argue with him. He went on in his way, and said that Our Lord needn't trouble to tell him that finally they remembered to which city they had come, and went to church barefooted and in penitents' garb. That spirit had, of course, not lasted long enough to be worth mentioning. And there-upon he leaned once more over the tower and pointed downward toward Jerusalem. He pointed out the Christians' camp outside the city. 'Do you see how your knights celebrate their victories?' he asked. And Our Lord saw that there was revelry everywhere in the camp. Knights and soldiers sat and looked upon Syrian dancers. Filled goblets went the rounds while they threw dice for the spoils of war and —"

"They listened to fools who told vile stories," interpolated Raniero. "Was not this also a great sin?"

The fool laughed and shook his head at Raniero, as much as to say, "Wait! I will pay you back."

"No, don't interrupt me!" he begged once again. "A poor fool forgets so easily what he would say. Ah! it was this: Saint Peter asked Our Lord if He thought these people were much of a credit to Him. To this, of course, Our Lord had to reply that He did not think they were.

" 'They were robbers and murderers before they left home, and robbers and murderers they are even today. This undertaking you could just as well have left undone. No good will come of it,' said Saint Peter."

"Come, come, fool!" said Raniero in a threatening tone. But the fool seemed to consider it an honour to test how far he could go without someone jumping up and throwing him out, and he continued fearlessly.

"Our Lord only bowed His head, like one who acknowledges that he is being justly rebuked. But almost at the same instant He leaned forward eagerly and peered down with closer scrutiny than before. Saint Peter also glanced down. 'What are you looking for?' he wondered."

The fool delivered this speech with much animated facial play. All the knights saw Our Lord and Saint Peter before their eyes, and they wondered what it was Our Lord had caught sight of.

"Our Lord answered that it was nothing in particular," said the fool. "Saint Peter gazed in the direction of Our Lord's glance, but he could discover nothing except that Our Lord sat and looked down into a big tent, outside which a couple of Saracen heads were set up on long lances, and where a lot of fine rugs, golden vessels, and costly weapons, captured in the Holy City, were piled up. In that tent they carried on as they did everywhere else in the camp. A company of knights sat and emptied their goblets. The only difference might be that here there were more drinking and roystering than elsewhere. Saint Peter could not comprehend why Our Lord was so pleased when he looked down there, that his eyes fairly sparkled with delight. So many hard and cruel faces he had rarely seen gathered around a drinking table. And he who was host at the board and sat at the head of the table was the most dreadful of all. He was a man of thirty-five, frightfully big and coarse, with a blowzy countenance covered with scars and scratches, calloused hands, and a loud, bellowing voice."

Here the fool paused a moment, as if he feared to go on, but both Raniero and the others liked to hear him talk of themselves, and only laughed at his audacity.

M

"You're a daring fellow," said Raniero, "so let us see what you are driving at!"

"Finally, Our Lord said a few words," continued the fool, "which made Saint Peter understand what he rejoiced over. He asked Saint Peter if He saw wrongly, or if it could actually be true that one of the knights had a burning candle beside him."

Raniero gave a start at these words. Now, at last, he was angry with the fool, and reached out his hand for a heavy wine pitcher to throw at his face, but he controlled himself that he might hear whether the fellow wished to speak to his credit or discredit.

"Saint Peter saw now," narrated the fool, "that although the tent was lighted mostly by torches, one of the knights really had a burning wax candle beside him. It was a long, thick candle, one of the sort made to burn twenty-four hours. The knight, who had no candlestick to set it in, had gathered together some stones and piled them around it, to make it stand."

The company burst into shrieks of laughter at this. All pointed at a candle which stood on the table beside Raniero, and was exactly like the one the fool had described. The blood mounted to Raniero's head; for this was the candle which he had a few hours before been permitted to light at the Holy Sepulchre. He had been unable to make up his mind to let it die out.

"When Saint Peter saw that candle," said the fool, "it dawned upon him what it was that Our Lord was so happy over, but at the same time he could not help feeling just a little sorry for Him. 'Oh,' he said, 'it was the same knight that leaped upon the wall this morning immediately after the gentleman of Boulogne, and who this evening was permitted to light his candle at the Holy Sepulchre ahead of all the others' — 'True!' said Our Lord. 'And, as you see, his candle is still burning'."

The fool talked very fast now, casting an occasional sly glance at

Raniero. "Saint Peter could not help pitying Our Lord. 'Can't you understand why he keeps that candle burning?' said he. 'You must not believe that he thinks of your sufferings and death whenever he looks at it. But he thinks only of the glory which he won when he was acknowledged to be the bravest man in the troop after Godfrey'."

At this all Raniero's guests laughed. Raniero was very angry, but he, too, forced himself to laugh. He knew they would have found it still more amusing if he hadn't been able to take a little fun.

"But Our Lord contradicted Saint Peter," said the fool. " 'Don't you see how careful he is with the light?' asked He. 'He puts his hand before the flame as soon as anyone raises the tent-flap for fear the draught will blow it out. And he is constantly occupied in chasing away the moths which fly around it and threaten to extinguish it'."

The laughter grew merrier and merrier, for what the fool said was the truth. Raniero found it more and more difficult to control himself. He felt he could not endure that anyone should jest about the sacred candle.

"Still, Saint Peter was dubious," continued the fool. "He asked Our Lord if He knew that knight. 'He's not one who goes often to Mass or wears out the prie-dieu,' said he. But Our Lord could not be swerved from His opinion.

" 'Saint Peter, Saint Peter,' He said earnestly. 'Remember that henceforth this knight shall become more pious than Godfrey. Whence do piety and gentleness spring, if not from my sepulchre? You shall see Raniero di Raniero help widows and distressed prisoners. You shall see him care for the sick and despairing as he now cares for the sacred candle-flame'."

At this they laughed inordinately. It struck them all as very ludicrous, for they knew Raniero's disposition and mode of living. But he himself found both the jokes and laughter intolerable. He sprang to his feet and wanted to reprove the fool. As he did this, he bumped so hard against the table — which was only a door set up on loose boxes — that it wobbled, and the candle fell down. It was evident now how careful Raniero was to keep the candle burning. He controlled his anger and gave himself time to pick it up and brighten the flame, before he rushed upon the fool. But when he had trimmed the light the fool had already darted out of the tent, and Raniero knew it would be useless to pursue him in the darkness. "I shall probably run across him another time," he thought, and sat down.

Meanwhile the guests had laughed mockingly, and one of them turned to Raniero and wanted to continue the jesting. He said: "There is one thing, however, which is certain, Raniero, and that is — this time you can't send to the Madonna in Florence the most precious things you have won in the battle."

Raniero asked why he thought that he should not follow his old habit this time.

"For no other reason," said the knight, "than that the most precious thing you have won is that sacred candle-flame, which you were permitted to light at the Church of the Holy Sepulchre in presence of the whole corps. Surely you can't send that to Florence!"

Again the other knights laughed, but Raniero was now in the mood to undertake the wildest projects, just to put an end to their laughter. He came to a conclusion quickly, called to an old squire, and said to him: "Make ready, Giovanni, for a long journey. Tomorrow you shall travel to Florence with this sacred candle-flame."

But the squire said a blunt no to this command. "This is something which I don't care to undertake," he said. "How should it be possible to travel to Florence with a candle-flame? It would be extinguished before I had left the camp."

Raniero asked one after another of his men. He received the same reply from all. They scarcely seemed to take his command seriously.

It was a foregone conclusion that the foreign knights who were his guests should laugh even louder and more merrily, as it became apparent that none of Raniero's men wished to carry out his order.

Raniero grew more and more excited. Finally he lost his patience and shouted: "This candle-flame shall nevertheless be borne to Florence; and since no one else will ride there with it, I will do so myself!"

"Consider before you promise anything of the kind!" said a knight. "You ride away from a principality."

"I swear to you that I will carry this sacred flame to Florence!" exclaimed Raniero. "I shall do what no one else has cared to undertake."

The old squire defended himself. "Master, it's another matter for you. You can take with you a large retinue but me you would send alone."

But Raniero was clean out of himself, and did not consider his words. "I, too, shall travel alone," said he.

But with this declaration Raniero had carried his point. Everyone in the tent had ceased laughing. Terrified, they sat and stared at him.

"Why don't you laugh any more?" asked Raniero. "This undertaking surely can't be anything but a child's game for a brave man."

III

The next morning at dawn Raniero mounted his horse. He was in full armour, but over it he had thrown a coarse pilgrim cloak, so that the iron dress should not become overheated by exposure to the sun's rays. He was armed with a sword and battle-club, and rode a good horse. He held in his hand a burning candle, and to the saddle he had tied a couple of bundles of long wax candles, so the flame should not die out for lack of nourishment.

Raniero rode slowly through the long, encumbered tent street, and thus far all went well. It was still so early that the mists which had arisen from the deep dales surrounding Jerusalem were not dispersed, and Raniero rode forward as in a white night. The whole troop slept, and Raniero passed the guards easily. None of them called out his name, for the mist prevented their seeing him, and the roads were covered with a dust-like soil a foot high, which made the horse's tramp inaudible.

Raniero was soon outside the camp and started on the road which led to Joppa. Here it was smoother, but he rode very slowly now, because of the candle, which burned feebly in the thick mist. Big insects kept dashing against the flame. Raniero had all he could do guarding it, but he was in the best of spirits and thought all the while that the mission which he had undertaken was so easy that a child could manage it.

Meanwhile, the horse grew weary of the slow pace, and began to trot. The flame began to flicker in the wind. It didn't help that Raniero tried to shield it with his hand and with the cloak. He saw that it was about to be extinguished.

But he had no desire to abandon the project so soon. He stopped the horse, sat still a moment, and pondered. Then he dismounted and tried sitting backwards, so that his body shielded the flame from the wind. In this way he succeeded in keeping it burning; but he realised now that the journey would be more difficult than he had thought at the beginning.

When he had passed the mountains which surround Jerusalem, the fog lifted. He rode forward now in the greatest solitude. There were no people, houses, green trees, nor plants — only bare rocks.

Here Raniero was attacked by robbers. They were idle folk, who followed the camp without permission, and lived by theft and plunder. They had lain in hiding behind a hill, and Raniero — who rode

182

backwards — had not seen them until they had surrounded him and brandished their swords at him.

There were about twelve men. They looked wretched, and rode poor horses. Raniero saw at once that it would not be difficult for him to break through this company and ride on. And after his proud boast of the night before, he was unwilling to abandon his undertaking easily.

He saw no other means of escape than to compromise with the robbers. He told them that, since he was armed and rode a good horse, it might be difficult to overpower him if he defended himself. And as he was bound by a vow, he did not wish to offer resistance, but they could take whatever they wanted, without a struggle, if only they promised not to put out his light.

The robbers had expected a hard struggle, and were very happy over Raniero's proposal, and began immediately to plunder him. They took from him armour and steed, weapons and money. The only thing they let him keep was the coarse cloak and the two bundles of wax candles. They sacredly kept their promise, also, not to put out the candle-flame.

One of them mounted Raniero's horse. When he noticed what a fine animal he was, he felt a little sorry for the rider. He called out to him: "Come, come, we must not be too cruel toward a Christian. You shall have my old horse to ride."

It was a miserable old screw of a horse. It moved as stiffly, and with as much difficulty, as if it were made of wood.

When the robbers had gone at last, and Raniero had mounted the wretched horse, he said to himself: "I must have become bewitched by this candle-flame. For its sake I must now travel along the roads like a crazy beggar."

He knew it would be wise for him to turn back, because the undertaking was really impracticable. But such an intense yearning to accomplish it had come over him that he could not resist the desire to go on. Therefore, he went farther. He saw all around him the same bare, yellowish hills.

After a while he came across a goatherd, who tended four goats. When Raniero saw the animals grazing on the barren ground, he wondered if they ate earth.

This goatherd had owned a larger flock, which had been stolen from him by the Crusaders. When he noticed a solitary Christian come riding toward him, he tried to do him all the harm he could. He rushed up to him and struck at his light with his staff. Raniero was so taken up by the flame that he could not defend himself even against a goatherd. He only drew the candle close to him to protect it. The goatherd struck at it several times more, then he paused, astonished, and ceased striking. He noticed that Raniero's cloak had caught fire, but Raniero did nothing to smother the blaze, so long as the sacred flame was in danger. The goatherd looked as though he felt ashamed. For a long time he followed Raniero and in one place, where the road was very narrow, with a deep chasm on each side of it, he came up and led the horse for him.

Raniero smiled and thought the goatherd surely regarded him as a holy man who had undertaken a voluntary penance.

Toward evening Raniero began to meet people. Rumours of the fall of Jerusalem had already spread to the coast, and a throng of people had immediately prepared to go up there. There were pilgrims who for years had awaited an opportunity to get into Jerusalem, also some newly-arrived troops; but they were mostly merchants who were hastening with provisions.

When these throngs met Raniero, who came riding backwards with a burning candle in his hand, they cried: "A madman, a madman!"

The majority were Italians; and Raniero heard how they shouted in his own tongue, "Pazzo, pazzo!" which means "a madman, a madman."

Raniero, who had been able to keep himself well in check all day, became intensely irritated by these ever-recurring shouts. Instantly he dismounted and began to chastise the offenders with his hard fists. When they saw how heavy the blows were, they took to their heels, and Raniero soon stood alone on the road.

Now Raniero was himself again. "In truth they were right to call me a madman," he said, as he looked around for the light. He did not know what he had done with it. At last he saw that it had rolled down into a hollow. The flame was extinguished, but he saw fire gleam from a dry grass-tuft close beside it, and understood that luck was with him, for the flame had ignited the grass before it had gone out.

"This might have been an inglorious end of a deal of trouble," he thought, as he lit the candle and stepped into the saddle. He was rather mortified. It did not seem to him very probable that his journey would be a success.

In the evening Raniero reached Ramle, and rode up to a place where caravans usually had night harbour. It was a large covered yard. All around it were little stalls where travellers could put up their horses. There were no rooms, but folk could sleep beside the animals.

The place was overcrowded with people, yet the host found room for Raniero and his horse. He also gave fodder to the horse and food to the rider.

When Raniero perceived that he was well treated, he thought: "I almost believe the robbers did me a service when they took from me my armour and my horse. I shall certainly get out of the country more easily with my light burden, if they mistake me for a lunatic."

When he had led the horse into the stall, he sat down on a sheaf of straw and held the candle in his hands. It was his intention not to fall asleep, but to remain awake all night. But he had hardly seated himself when he fell asleep. He was fearfully exhausted, and in his sleep he stretched out full length and did not wake till morning.

When he awoke he saw neither flame nor candle. He searched in the straw for the candle, but did not find it anywhere.

"Someone has taken it from me and extinguished it," he said. He tried to persuade himself that he was glad that all was over, and that he need not pursue an impossible undertaking.

But as he pondered, he felt a sense of emptiness and loss. He thought that never before had he so longed to succeed in anything on which he had set his mind.

He led the horse out and groomed and saddled it.

When he was ready to set out, the host who owned the caravan-serai came up to him with a burning candle. He said in Frankish: "When you fell asleep last night, I had to take your light from you, but here you have it again."

Raniero betrayed nothing, but said very calmly: "It was wise of you to extinguish it."

"I have not extinguished it," said the man. "I noticed that it was burning when you arrived, and I thought it was of importance to you that it should continue to burn. If you see how much it has decreased, you will understand that it has been burning all night."

Raniero beamed with happiness. He commended the host heartily, and rode away in the best of spirits.

IV

When Raniero broke away from the camp at Jerusalem, he intended to travel from Joppa to Italy by sea, but changed his mind after he had been robbed of his money, and decided to make the journey by land.

It was a long journey. From Joppa he went northward along the Syrian coast. Then he rode westward along the peninsula of Asia Minor, then northward again, all the way to Constantinople. From there he still had a monotonously long distance to travel to reach Florence. During the whole journey Raniero had lived upon the contributions of the pious. They that shared their bread with him mostly were pilgrims who at this time travelled *en masse* to Jerusalem.

Regardless of the fact that he nearly always rode alone, his days were neither long nor monotonous. He must always guard the candle-flame, and on its account he never could feel at ease. It needed only a puff of breeze — a raindrop — and there would have been an end to it.

As Raniero rode over lonely roads, and thought only about keeping the flame alive, it occurred to him that once before he had been concerned with something similar. Once before he had seen a person watch over something which was just as sensitive as a candle-flame.

This recollection was so vague to him at first that he wondered if it was something he had dreamed.

But as he rode on alone through the country, it kept recurring to him that he had participated in something similar once before.

"It is as if all my life long I had heard tell of nothing else," said he.

One evening he rode into a city. It was after sundown, and the housewives stood in their doorways and watched for their husbands. Then he noticed one who was tall and slender, and had earnest eyes. She reminded him of Francesca degli Uberti.

Instantly it became clear to him what he had been pondering over. It came to him that for Francesca her love must have been as a sacred flame which she had always wished to keep burning, and which she had constantly feared that Raniero would quench. He was astonished at this thought, but grew more and more certain that the matter stood thus. For the first time he began to understand why Francesca had left him, and that it was not with feats of arms he should win her back.

The journey which Raniero made was of long duration. This was in part due to the fact that he could not venture out when the weather was bad. Then he sat in some caravanserai, and guarded the candle-flame. These were very trying days.

One day, when he rode over Mount Lebanon, he saw that a storm was brewing. He was riding high up among awful precipices, and a frightful distance from any human abode. Finally he saw on the summit of a rock the tomb of a Saracen saint. It was a little square stone structure with a vaulted roof. He thought it best to seek shelter there.

He had barely entered when a snowstorm came up, which raged for two days and nights. At the same time it grew so cold that he came near freezing to death.

Raniero knew that there were heaps of branches and twigs out on the mountain, and it would not have been difficult for him to gather fuel for a fire. But he considered the candle-flame which he carried very sacred, and did not wish to light anything from it, except the candles before the Blessed Virgin's Altar.

The storm increased, and at last he heard thunder and saw gleams of lightning.

Then came a flash which struck the mountain, just in front of the tomb, and set fire to a tree. And in this way he was enabled to light his fire without having to borrow of the sacred flame.

As Raniero was riding on through a desolate portion of the Cilician mountain district, his candles were all used up. The candles which

189

he had brought with him from Jerusalem had long since been consumed; but still he had been able to manage because he had found Christian communities all along the way, of whom he had begged fresh candles.

But now his resources were exhausted, and he thought that this would be the end of his journey.

When the candle was so nearly burnt out that the flame scorched his hand, he jumped from his horse and gathered branches and dry leaves and lit these with the last of the flame. But up on the mountain there was very little that would ignite, and the fire would soon burn out.

While he sat and grieved because the sacred flame must die, he heard singing down the road, and a procession of pilgrims came marching up the steep path, bearing candles in their hands. They were on their way to a grotto where a holy man had lived, and Raniero followed them. Among them was a woman who was very old and had difficulty in walking, and Raniero carried her up the mountain.

When she thanked him afterwards, he made a sign to her that she should give him her candle. She did so, and several others also presented him with the candles which they carried. He extinguished the candles, hurried down the steep path, and lit one of them with the last spark from the fire lighted by the sacred flame.

One day at the noon hour it was very warm, and Raniero had lain down to sleep in a thicket. He slept soundly, and the candle stood beside him between a couple of stones. When he had been asleep a while, it began to rain, and this continued for some time, without his waking. When at last he was startled out of his sleep, the ground around him was wet, and he hardly dared glance toward the light, for fear it might be quenched.

But the light burned calmly and steadily in the rain, and Raniero saw that this was because two little birds flew and fluttered just above the flame. They caressed it with their bills, and held their wings outspread, and in this way they protected the sacred flame from the rain.

He took off his hood immediately, and hung it over the candle. Thereupon he reached out his hand for the two little birds, for he had been seized with a desire to pet them. Neither of them flew away because of him, and he could catch them.

He was very much astonished that the birds were not afraid of him. "It is because they know I have no thought except to protect that which is the most sensitive of all, that they do not fear me," thought he.

191

Raniero rode in the vicinity of Nicaea, in Bithynia. Here he met some western gentlemen who were conducting a party of recruits to the Holy Land. In this company was Robert Taillefer, who was a wandering knight and a troubadour.

Raniero, in his torn cloak, came riding along with the candle in his hand, and the warriors began as usual to shout, "A madman, a madman!"

But Robert silenced them, and addressed the rider. "Have you journeyed far in this manner?" he asked.

"I have ridden like this all the way from Jerusalem," answered Raniero.

"Has your light been extinguished many times during the journey?"

"Still burns the flame that lighted the candle with which I rode away from Jerusalem," responded Raniero.

Then Robert Taillefer said to him : "I am also one of those who carry a light, and I would that it burned always. But perchance you, who have brought your light burning all the way from Jerusalem, can tell me what I shall do that it may not become extinguished?"

Then Raniero answered: "Master, it is a difficult task, although it appears to be of slight importance. This little flame demands of you that you shall entirely cease to think of anything else. It will not allow you to have any sweetheart — in case you should desire anything of the sort — neither would you dare on account of this flame to sit down at a revel. You cannot have aught else in your thoughts than just this flame, and must possess no other happiness. But my chief reason for advising you against making the journey which I have weathered is that you cannot for an instant feel secure. It matters not through how many perils you may have guarded the flame, you cannot for an instant think yourself secure, but must ever expect that the very next moment it may fail you."

But Robert Taillefer raised his head proudly and answered: "What you have done for your sacred flame I may do for mine."

Raniero arrived in Italy. One day he rode through lonely roads up among the mountains. A woman came running after him and begged him to give her a light from his candle. "The fire in my hut is out," said she. "My children are hungry. Give me a light that I may heat my oven and bake bread for them!"

She reached for the burning candle, but Raniero held it back because he did not wish that anything should be lighted by that flame but the candles before the image of the Blessed Virgin.

Then the woman said to him: "Pilgrim, give me a light, for the life of my children is the flame which I am in duty bound to keep burning!" And because of these words he permitted her to light the wick of her lamp from his flame.

Several hours later he rode into a town. It lay far up on the mountain, where it was very cold. A peasant stood in the road and saw the poor wretch who came riding in his torn cloak. Instantly he stripped off the short mantle which he wore, and flung it to him. But the mantle fell directly over the candle and extinguished the flame.

Then Raniero remembered the woman who had borrowed a light of him. He turned back to her and had his candle lighted anew with sacred fire.

When he was ready to ride farther, he said to her: "You say that the sacred flame which you must guard is the life of your children. Can you tell me what name this candle's flame bears, which I have carried over long roads?"

"Where was your candle lighted?" asked the woman.

"It was lighted at Christ's sepulchre," said Raniero.

"Then it can only be called Gentleness and Love of Humanity," said she.

Raniero laughed at the answer. He thought himself a singular apostle of virtues such as these.

Raniero rode forward between beautiful blue hills. He saw he was near Florence. He was thinking that he must soon part with his light. He thought of his tent in Jerusalem, which he had left filled with trophies, and the brave soldiers who were still in Palestine, and who would be glad to have him take up the business of war once more, and bear them on to new conquests and honours.

Then he perceived that he experienced no pleasure in thinking of this, but that his thoughts were drawn in another direction.

Then he realized for the first time that he was no longer the same man that had gone from Jerusalem. The ride with the sacred flame had compelled him to rejoice with all who were peaceable and wise and compassionate, and to abhor the savage and warlike.

He was happy every time he thought of people who laboured peacefully in their homes, and it occurred to him that he would willingly move into his old workshop in Florence and do beautiful and artistic work.

"Verily this flame has re-created me," he thought. "I believe it has made a new man of me."

V

It was Eastertide when Raniero rode into Florence. He had scarcely come in through the city gate — riding backwards, with his hood drawn down over his face and the burning candle in his hand — when a beggar arose and shouted the customary "Pazzo, pazzo!"

At this cry a street gamin darted out of a doorway, and a loafer, who had had nothing else to do for a long time than to lie and gaze at

194

the clouds, jumped to his feet. Both began shouting the same thing: "Pazzo, pazzo!"

Now that there were three who shrieked, they made a good deal of noise and so woke up all the street urchins. They came rushing out from nooks and corners. As soon as they saw Raniero, in his torn coat, on the wretched horse, they shouted: "Pazzo, pazzo!"

But this was only what Raniero was accustomed to. He rode quietly up the street, seeming not to notice the shouters.

Then they were not content with merely shouting, but one of them jumped up and tried to blow out the light. Raniero raised the candle on high, trying at the same time to prod his horse, to escape the boys.

They kept even pace with him, and did everything they could to put out the light.

The more he exerted himself to protect the flame the more excited they became. They leaped upon one another's backs, puffed their cheeks out, and blew. They flung their caps at the candle. It was only because they were so numerous and crowded on one another that they did not succeed in quenching the flame.

This was the largest procession on the street. People stood at the windows and laughed. No one felt any sympathy with a madman, who wanted to defend his candle-flame. It was church hour, and many worshippers were on their way to Mass. They, too, stopped and laughed at the sport.

But now Raniero stood upright in the saddle, so that he could shield the candle. He looked wild. The hood had fallen back and they saw his face, which was wasted and pale, like a martyr's. The candle he held uplifted as high as he could.

The entire street was one great swarm of people. Even the older ones began to take part in the play. The women waved their head-shawls and the men swung their caps. Everyone worked to extinguish the light.

Raniero rode under the vine-covered balcony of a house. Upon this stood a woman. She leaned over the lattice-work, snatched the candle, and ran in with it. The woman was Francesca degli Uberti.

The whole populace burst into shrieks of laughter and shouts, but Raniero swayed in his saddle and fell to the street.

As soon as he lay there stricken and unconscious, the street was emptied of people.

No one wished to take charge of the fallen man. His horse was the only creature that stopped beside him.

As soon as the crowds had got away from the street, Francesca degli Uberti came out from her house, with the burning candle in her hand. She was still pretty; her features were gentle, and her eyes were deep and earnest.

She went up to Raniero and bent over him. He lay senseless, but the instant the candle light fell upon his face, he moved and roused himself. It was apparent that the candle-flame had complete power over him. When Francesca saw that he had regained his senses, she said: "Here is your candle. I snatched it from you, as I saw how anxious you were to keep it burning. I knew of no other way to help you."

Raniero had had a bad fall, and was hurt. But now nothing could hold him back. He began to raise himself slowly. He wanted to walk, but wavered, and was about to fall. Then he tried to mount his horse. Francesca helped him. "Where do you wish to go?" she asked when he sat in the saddle again. "I want to go to the cathedral," he answered. "Then I shall accompany you," she said, "for I'm going to Mass." And she led the horse for him.

Francesca had recognized Raniero the very moment she saw him, but he did not see who she was, for he did not take time to notice her. He kept his gaze fixed upon the candle-flame alone.

They were absolutely silent all the way. Raniero thought only of the flame, and of guarding it well these last moments. Francesca could not speak, for she felt she did not wish to be certain of that which she feared. She could not believe but that Raniero had come home insane. Although she was almost certain of this, she would rather not speak with him, in order to avoid any positive assurance.

After a while Raniero heard someone weep near him. He looked around and saw that it was Francesca degli Uberti, who walked beside him; and she wept. But Raniero saw her only for an instant, and said nothing to her. He wanted to think only of the sacred flame.

Raniero let her conduct him to the sacristy. There he dismounted. He thanked Francesca for her help, but looked all the while not upon her, but on the light. He walked alone up to the priests in the sacristy.

Francesca went into the church. It was Easter Eve, and all the candles stood unlighted upon the altars, as a symbol of mourning. Francesca thought that every flame of hope which had ever burned within her was now extinguished.

In the church there was profound solemnity. There were many priests at the altar. The canons sat in a body in the chancel, with the bishop among them.

By and by Francesca noticed there was commotion among the priests. Nearly all who were not needed to serve at Mass arose and went out into the sacristy. Finally, the bishop went too.

When Mass was over, a priest stepped up to the chancel railing and began to speak to the people. He related that Raniero di Raniero had arrived in Florence with sacred fire from Jerusalem. He narrated what the rider had endured and suffered on the way. And he praised him exceeding much.

The people sat spellbound and listened to this. Francesca had never before experienced such a blissful moment. "O God!" she sighed, "this is greater happiness than I can bear." Her tears fell as she listened.

The priest talked long and well. Finally he said in a strong, thrilling voice: "It may perchance appear like a trivial thing now, that a candle-flame had been brought to Florence. But I say to you: Pray God that He will send Florence many bearers of Eternal Light; then she will become a great power, and be extolled as a city among cities!"

When the priest had finished speaking, the entrance doors of the church were thrown open, and a procession of canons and monks and priests marched up the centre aisle toward the altar. The bishop came last, and by his side walked Raniero, in the same cloak that he had worn during the entire journey.

But when Raniero had crossed the threshold of the cathedral, an old man arose and walked toward him. It was Oddo, the father of the journeyman who had once worked for Raniero, and had hanged himself because of him.

When this man had come up to the bishop and Raniero, he bowed to them. Thereupon he said in such a loud voice that all in the church heard him: "It is a great thing for Florence that Raniero has come with sacred fire from Jerusalem. Such a thing has never before been heard of or conceived. For that reason perhaps there may be many who will say that it is not possible Therefore, I beg that all the people may know what proofs and witnesses Raniero has brought with him, to assure us that this is actually fire which was lighted in Jerusalem."

When Raniero heard this he said: "God help me! how can I produce witnesses? I have made the journey alone. Deserts and mountain wastes must come and testify for me."

"Raniero is an honest knight," said the bishop, "and we believe him on his word."

"Raniero must know himself that doubts will arise as to this," said Oddo. "Surely, he cannot have ridden entirely alone. His little pages could certainly testify for him."

Then Francesca degli Uberti rushed up to Raniero. "Why need we witnesses?" said she. "All the women in Florence would swear on oath that Raniero speaks the truth!"

Then Raniero smiled, and his countenance brightened for a moment. Thereupon he turned his thoughts and his gaze once more upon the candle-flame.

There was great commotion in the church. Some said that Raniero should not be allowed to light the candles on the altar until his claim was substantiated. With this many of his old enemies sided.

Then Jacopo degli Uberti rose and spoke on Raniero's behalf. "I believe everyone here knows that no very great friendship has existed between my son-in-law and me," he said ; "but now both my sons and I will answer for him. We believe he has performed this task, and we know that one who has been disposed to carry out such an undertaking is a wise, discreet, and noble-minded man, whom we are glad to receive among us."

But Oddo and many others were not disposed to let him taste of the bliss he was yearning for. They got together in a close group and it was easy to see that they did not care to withdraw their demand.

Raniero apprehended that if this should develop into a fight, they would immediately try to get at the candle. As he kept his eyes steadily fixed upon his opponents, he raised the candle as high as he could.

He looked exhausted in the extreme, and distraught. One could see that, although he wished to hold out to the very last, he expected defeat. What mattered it to him now if he were permitted to light the candles? Oddo's word had been a death-blow. When doubt was once awakened, it would spread and increase. He fancied that Oddo had already extinguished the sacred flame for ever.

A little bird came fluttering through the great open doors into the church. It flew straight into Raniero's light. He hadn't time to snatch it aside, and the bird dashed against it and put out the flame.

Raniero's arm dropped, and tears sprang to his eyes. The first moment he felt this as a sort of relief. It was better thus than if human beings had killed it.

The little bird continued its flight into the church, fluttering confusedly hither and thither, as birds do when they come into a room.

Simultaneously a loud cry resounded throughout the church: "The bird is on fire! The sacred candle-flame has set its wings on fire!"

The little bird chirped anxiously. For a few moments it fluttered about, like a flickering flame, under the high chancel arches. Then it sank suddenly, dropped dead upon the Madonna's Altar.

But the moment the bird fell upon the Altar, Raniero was standing there. He had forced his way through the church, no one had been able to stop him. From the sparks which destroyed the bird's wings he lit the candles before the Madonna's Altar.

Then the bishop raised his staff and proclaimed: "God willed it! God has testified for him!"

And all the people in the church, both his friends and opponents, abandoned their doubts and conjectures. They cried as with one voice, transported by God's miracle: "God willed it! God has testified for him!"

Of Raniero there is now only a legend, which says he enjoyed great good fortune for the remainder of his days, and was wise, and prudent, and compassionate. But the people of Florence always called him Pazzo degli Raniero, in remembrance of the fact that they had believed him insane. And this became his honorary title. He founded a dynasty, which was named Pazzi, and is called so even to this day.

It might also be worth mentioning that it became a custom in Florence, each year at Easter Eve, to celebrate a festival in memory of

Raniero's home-coming with the sacred flame, and that, on this occasion, they always let an artificial bird fly with fire through the church. This festival would most likely have been celebrated even in our day had not some changes taken place recently.

But if it be true, as many hold, that the bearers of sacred fire who have lived in Florence and have made the city one of the most glorious on earth, have taken Raniero as their model, and have thereby been encouraged to sacrifice, to suffer and endure, this may here be left untold.

For what has been done by this light, which in dark times has gone out from Jerusalem, can neither be measured nor counted.

Selma Lagerlöf

Selma Ottilia Lovisa Lagerlöf was born in Värmland, Sweden, on November 20, 1858, and died there on March 16, 1940. During her lifetime she received considerable fame as a novelist, was translated into several languages, and had a film made of her extraordinary book *The Ferryman of Death*. She was the first woman to receive the Nobel Prize for Literature and to be admitted into the select membership of the Swedish Academy. This success enabled her to buy and reconstruct her parents' estate, her beloved Mårbacka, and to pass the rest of her life writing in the thickly wooded hill country of Värmland, where her ancestors had lived for centuries.

In her third year she suffered what was apparently a form of infantile paralysis which meant that throughout her childhood she needed special care. Cut off from taking part in the usual children's games she enjoyed many hours with her grandmother who told her the most wonderful fairy stories. Later she recalled the blow her grandmother's death dealt to her when, at the age of five, it seemed that a magic world was closed for ever. Part of her life's task was to reopen that magic door, not only for herself, but for a wider circle of readers.

Selma read a great deal as a child. She confessed to having finished all of Sir Walter Scott by the time she was ten. During her adolescence she began to write poetry. As a twenty-one-year-old bridesmaid she gave an inspired wedding oration which deeply impressed a wedding guest with some literary connections. Hopes of having her poetry published, however, came to nothing, and this finally led to her resolve to train as a school teacher in Stockholm. The capital offered wider literary and intellectual horizons, and she discovered the prose of Thomas Carlyle which helped her to form the style of her early novels.

She worked hard as a teacher and continued to write for ten long years before her work came to the attention of the Danish critic Georg Brandes, who had done so much to make the public aware of Strindberg and Nietzsche. The publication of her first novel *The Story of Gösta Berling* in 1891 was a turning point in her life. In her thirty-third year her genius was at last recognized and she was awarded a travelling scholarship by the Swedish crown. After finishing her anti-socialist novel *The Miracles of Antichrist*, she visited the Holy Land to do research for her remarkable *Jerusalem*, which was a new departure in literary form, moving freely between Sweden and Palestine, covering a vast range of human experience. The atmosphere of the Holy Land began to activate the buried memories of her grandmother's stories. Although she could only recall one of the stories in detail, the magic door began to open again. In 1904 her most truly international book *Christ Legends* appeared.